Creating the Joyful Writer

Introducing the Holistic Approach in the Classroom

Susan A. Schiller

Rowman & Littlefield Education
Lanham, Maryland • Toronto • Plymouth, UK
2007

Published in the United States of America
by Rowman & Littlefield Education
A Division of Rowman & Littlefield Publishers, Inc.
A wholly owned subsidiary of The Rowman & Littlefield Publishing Group, Inc.
4501 Forbes Boulevard, Suite 200, Lanham, Maryland 20706
www.rowmaneducation.com

Estover Road
Plymouth PL6 7PY
United Kingdom

Copyright © 2007 by Susan A. Schiller

All rights reserved. No part of this publication may be reproduced, stored in a retrieval system, or transmitted in any form or by any means, electronic, mechanical, photocopying, recording, or otherwise, without the prior permission of the publisher.

British Library Cataloguing in Publication Information Available

Library of Congress Cataloging-in-Publication Data

Schiller, Susan A.
　Creating the joyful writer : introducing the holistic approach in the classroom / Susan Schiller.
　　p. cm.
　Includes bibliographical references.
　ISBN-13: 978-1-57886-632-8 (hardcover : alk. paper)
　ISBN-10: 1-57886-632-4 (hardcover : alk. paper)
　ISBN-13: 978-1-57886-633-5 (pbk. : alk. paper)
　ISBN-10: 1-57886-633-2 (pbk. : alk. paper)
　1. English language—Composition and exercises. 2. Creative thinking—Study and teaching. 3. Holistic education. I. Title.
　LB1576.S3253 2007
　428.0071—dc22

2007014018

∞™ The paper used in this publication meets the minimum requirements of American National Standard for Information Sciences—Permanence of Paper for Printed Library Materials, ANSI/NISO Z39.48-1992.
Manufactured in the United States of America.

This book is dedicated to special teachers who taught me to love learning:

Mrs. Fuller, 1st grade, Gregory Elementary School
Mrs. Streets, 3rd grade, Stockbridge Elementary School
Mr. Koljonen, 12th-grade German teacher, Thurston High School
Sr. Barbara Johns, Dr. Lynn Schaeffer, Dr. Maureen DesRoches, and Dr. Frank Rashid, Marygrove College
Dr. John Brereton, Dr. Barbara Couture, and Dr. Ruth Ray, Wayne State University

Contents

Preface *Jack P. Miller*		vii
Acknowledgments		ix
Introduction		xi
1	Background and Influential People	1
2	Creativity: A Holistic Route to Writing	14
3	Contemplating Great Things in Soul and Place	23
4	Walking in the Spirit of the Medicine Wheel: Learning to See What We Normally Do Not See	31
5	Write Your Own Ending	39
6	The Connected Self	42
7	Visioning in Silent Community	48
8	Screenplay Writing	51
9	Info-Commercial	55
10	Cave Art: Is It Literature? Is It Writing?	59
11	Finding Your Community's Literature	63
12	Creating a Life's Legacy	68
13	Music and Dance to Inspire the Pen	74

14	The Writer's Scrapbook	79
15	Voice and Identity: The Sound of Respect	83
16	Writing the Outdoors: 3 Days in Nature	89
Appendix A	Selected Holistic Schools	103
Appendix B	Rhetorical Aims and Organizational Strategies	109
Annotated Bibliography		113
About the Author		121

Preface
Jack P. Miller

In the day of No Child Left Behind, literacy has become a priority in education. Unfortunately, with an emphasis on standardized testing, many approaches to reading and writing are often mechanical as teachers "teach to the test." These approaches may, in fact, boost test scores in the short term, but we might ask, What do they lead to in the long term? Do current approaches really encourage a love of reading and writing in our students? As Susan A. Schiller, PhD, suggests at the beginning of her book, students are often given writing assignments disconnected from their lives and, as a result, there is little engagement in the writing process.

Dr. Schiller has developed an approach to writing that engages students holistically, as she believes, in her words, that students "should have the opportunity to use their intellect, their emotion, their spiritual side, their social abilities, and their physical skills; and they should have the opportunity to stretch their awareness of self, of community, and of the world." For Schiller, writing should be connected to the student's personal talents and interests.

Professor Schiller grounds her work within a holistic perspective, which is outlined at the beginning of this book, and thus develops a framework for the writing exercises that comprise most of the text. These exercises are designed for the students who Dr. Schiller works with at the postsecondary level, but I believe they could also be adapted to secondary school classrooms. The exercises are teacher friendly, as step-by-step guidelines are presented. They also include a variety of techniques, such as visualization to stimulate the student's imagination. A number of topics are covered in 14 chapters and include nature, identity, music and dance, screenplay writing, and community.

This book is clearly grounded in Susan Schiller's years of working with these exercises, and teachers using this book can feel confident about using them in their own classrooms. Dr. Schiller has shown us a way that we can truly engage students in the writing process and also assist their self-awareness and growth as people.

Acknowledgments

I wish to thank Jennifer Kaiser, whose enthusiastic faith in this project has motivated me more than she knows. The conversations and trips we have shared in the pursuit of understanding holistic education more thoroughly are even more important to me than the large amount of data she provided for the brief chronology in Chapter 2. A special thanks goes to Theopolis Gilmore, whose constant faith and love have supported me during this project and others.

Don Backus, Robert Root, Lori Rogers, and Pam Gates are colleagues who have shared expertise and advice throughout the writing of this text. Their encouragement means a great deal. Other inspiring people include Clint Burhans, Janae Goodchild, Carrie Lake, Carrie Jones, Stephanie Peck, Elizabeth Shamus, Nikki Frazier, Samantha Clark, Tessa Holman, Joel D'Annunzio, Kelly Stevens, and Emily Homrich. In addition, I want to acknowledge the people who organize the International Holistic Education Conference: Breaking New Ground. Their work stands as a beacon to educators who seek fresh approaches to learning and teaching.

Introduction

Holistic education addresses the whole person within a social and environmental context and perceives all elements of a person—intellectual, physical, emotional, social, and spiritual—as avenues for growth and learning. Holism also moves beyond conventional approaches that primarily value and rely on logical ways of knowing, ways that condition people to become competitors and consumers. Within educational settings writing is a natural site for holism because writing is a way of knowing that connects and draws from our inner and outer worlds.

It is time for writing instructors to bring joy back into the activity and for students to unlearn any of the negative attitudes they may have developed due to conventional approaches. When people write they should have the opportunity to use their intellects, their emotions, their spiritual sides, their social abilities, and their physical skills, and they should have the opportunity to stretch their awarenesses of self, of community, and of the world. Interconnections should arise naturally. Writers should make choices based on their personal preferences, talents, and interests. Self-satisfaction and effectiveness of the written document should lead any evaluation measures, if they are needed. Grades, or in other words, a reliance on comparisons and competition with others, should be avoided whenever possible.

Exigence and creativity should guide all the rhetorical choices, from word choice, to voice, to goal, to final version. Intuition and emotions should inform the writer and be considered respectful avenues of discovery. The intellect should be blended with emotions and physical ways of finding language. The writer should share with other people and seek social solutions to blocks that may arise along the writing path. Writing needs to be reconceptualized so that it may always be seen as an activity of positive and creative energy. It needs to be an activity based on and connected to something in the writer's world that allows the writing to be both *desirable* and *worthwhile* to that person.

Within most conventional schools and colleges, there is some pressure on teachers to promote what is commonly referred to as "academic writing or academic discourse." This usually means a researched topic, a persuasive aim, a formal voice, and a high degree of critical thinking. Yet, without equal attention given to multiple ways of knowing, including spiritual and emotional intelligence, an imbalance occurs and holistic learning does not emerge.

Moreover, current testing mandates at the state and federal levels encourage the imbalance and, by so doing, severely thwart self-development and creativity in both teachers and students. In fact, as Peter Elbow likes to remind me, "the structures in mainstream conventional schools often make it harder for good teachers and often do not give them the institutional support they need" (personal communication, February 12, 2007). Teachers and students need a change. It is time for a holistic approach to writing—one that allows the fullest possible range of opportunity for creativity and self-development.

Jane Tompkins (1996), in *A Life in School: What the Teacher Learned*, calls for a "more holistic approach to learning, a disciplinary training for people who teach in college that takes into account the fact that we are educators of whole human beings, a form of higher education that would take responsibility for the emergence of an integrated person" (p. 218). This book takes a step in that direction by providing a holistic approach that fosters creativity and joy in the doing and producing of written expression. It is not a grammar handbook or a traditional rhetoric or reader but could be used in conjunction with those types of texts. Chapters 1 and 2 are useful for providing background, history, and philosophical reasons for holistic education. While these are helpful to set the context for understanding the motivations driving the rest of the book, writing activities described in subsequent chapters can be experienced prior to reading these early chapters.

Chapter 1 describes holistic education and its historical pioneers. Chapter 2 suggests that teachers and learners should value and use creativity (rather than analysis) as a primary learning strategy. This chapter supports the amount of value placed on creativity in all of the subsequent chapters. Chapters 3 through 16 present holistic learning activities that provide a context and exigence for writing. Creativity, visual arts, and rhetorical decision making shape the majority of these activities, but all activities attempt to establish a context that provides learners with opportunities to use multiple intelligences. Some of the activities can be completed by individuals writing alone, but many require collaboration among partners or small groups. Step-by-step instructions, prerequisites, safety precautions, materials needed, time desired, and learning goals are also suggested. Most of these activities are flexible and can be easily altered to suit varying ages or skill levels and can be teacher directed or self-directed.

At the 2003 conference on holistic education, keynote speaker Satish Kumar called to holistic educators to focus on a trinity—soil, soul, and society—as a means to organize holistic education. From his viewpoint, these "can inspire a truly holistic thinking. They can bring nature, humanity and spirituality together" (Kumar, 2002, p. 75). Soil comes first because everything we have on Earth comes from the soil. It is our role to nourish, care, and preserve the soil in a way that sustains life on our planet. Next, we need to replenish our soul because with a vital soul, we can give to the Earth and society and know how best to receive gifts from both. Third, we must develop a society based on receiving and giving so that our lives are enriched (Kumar, 2002).

The activities presented in this book blend aspects of the trinity suggested by Kumar and move away from a focus on organizational strategies as is commonly done in conventional writing instruction. Appendixes A and B serve as resource material, and an annotated bibliography of suggested reading concludes this book. Teachers using this book need to be familiar with holistic principles. Background information is especially helpful if a teacher within a mainstream educational environment should need to explain or justify pedagogical decisions. The nonsectarian spiritual center of any holistic approach asks that teachers thus engaged have a personal commitment to their own spiritual and self-development.

REFERENCES

Kumar, S. (2002). *You are, therefore I am: A declaration of dependence.* Devon, England: Green Books.

Tompkins, J. (1996). *A life in school: What the teacher learned.* Reading, MA: Perseus.

CHAPTER 1

Background and Influential People

WHAT IS HOLISTIC EDUCATION?

Holistic education is generally perceived as an alternate form of education that concerns the whole learner. Holistic educators believe that the learner's intellect, emotions, physical body, spirit, and social nature develop together rather than independently and that drawing from the whole person is necessary to initiate deep and permanent learning experiences. It is believed that an imbalance occurs in our development if we use one part of our beings and not the others. For example, consider the person who exercises only the upper body. He or she might have great strength in the arms but lack the endurance needed to walk more than a mile.

Holistic education attempts to integrate all the ways of learning available to us. Inherent social and spiritual characteristics create the context within which the mind, emotion, and body are integrated. With this wholeness, one's spirit assumes a central and vital role because it is the source of our motivation for growth and learning. It is no surprise, then, that the learner is not seen as an independent agent but rather as a part of the greater whole that includes the family, the community, the natural environment, and the universe (Rocha, 2003). Holistic educators use wholeness as a means through which to teach, and they create methods through which wholeness fosters our full awareness. Our inner and outer lives are no longer isolated but integrated so that we come to a meaningful understanding of our spirits and our souls.

All around the world today, explorative educators are turning to holism as a means to evoke and recover the spiritual centers in learners that motivates, awakens, enlivens, and instigates creativity, compassion, honesty, fairness, responsibility, and respect (Lantieri, 2001). Ron Miller's (1997) *What Are Schools For?* presents a historical overview of the socioeconomic and political pressures that shaped most of the current purposes in mainstream public education, as well as those educators who sought and created alternative holistic systems for learners.

The timeline at the end of this chapter presents a chronological overview of people and ideas in holistic education. John P. Miller's *Holistic Teacher* (1993), *The Holistic Curriculum* (1996), and *Education and the Soul* (2000) extends the discussion and features the spiritual core quite emphatically. In 1997, Regina Paxton Foehr and I edited a collection, *The Spiritual Side of Writing: Releasing the Learner's Whole Potential*, aimed at teachers of writing in public institutions, which profiled ways a spiritual approach to teaching can occur without violating the national mandate to separate church and state. Rachael Kessler's *The Soul of Education* (2000) has been warmly embraced by educators, and her Passage Ways Institute offers training sessions for educators who wish to move toward a spiritual approach to teaching. Although inspired by wisdom traditions, her work at the institute seeks to remain as neutral as possible so that all worldviews are respected. For example, she offers "solo time" as an alternative practice to meditation in the classroom. During solo time, students are invited to spend time together in silence and stillness with freedom to choose how to be with that silence rather than following specific instructions.

In 2001 Linda Lantieri's edited collection *Schools With Spirit* argued for and provided examples of schools and educators who are successfully placing spirituality at the center of their educational approaches. According to Lantieri (2001), "spiritual experiences can be described as the conscious recognition of a connection that goes beyond our own minds or emotions. It's the kind of experience that sometimes leaves us without words to describe it" (p. 8).

While most people relegate spiritual experiences to sites outside the classroom, holistic educators agree that learners also need opportunities for spiritual experience inside the classroom. Creating learning experiences that evoke the sacred, defined by Parker Palmer as "that which is worthy of respect" (as cited in Lantieri, 2001, p. xiv), is a primary goal among holistic educators. Palmer's seminal book, *The Courage to Teach* (1998), is probably by far the most widely read book that advocates a spiritual approach to teaching and learning. Holistic educators believe that the spiritual—the sacred—is not isolated to religious systems but is indeed infused in all daily life, particularly in the soul of the learner. It only needs awakening.

HISTORICAL PEOPLE

The roots of holistic education and philosophy date from Jean-Jacques Rousseau, who lived from 1712 to 1778. He observed that child development proceeds at its own natural pace, which he argued, must be respected because "the first impulses of nature are always right; there is no original sin in the human heart" (as cited in R. Miller, 1997, p. 93). Rousseau also believed that the "creative power of the universe . . . God" (R. Miller, p. 9) is the source of the human personality. Therefore, the human spirit should be respected and included in education. He valued the learner's natural pace of learning and placed it at the heart of holistic education. Philosophers and education reformers who followed added to Rousseau's principles and argued for changes that would put the learner at the center and within social experiences that used the whole person rather than just the rational intellect.

The Swiss reformer Johann Pestalozzi (1746–1827) created boarding schools that featured farm life. Students lived and worked on farms, and all their learning drew from experiences this environment allowed. Like Rousseau, he also was adamant about teachers' respecting students' experiences. Pestalozzi's school became world famous, and educators from various parts of the world came to observe and study his method (R. Miller, 1997). A German reformer who worked with Pestalozzi, Friedrich Froebel, went on to create the kindergarten.

In early America, transcendentalists Ralph Waldo Emerson, Henry David Thoreau, William Ellery Channing, George Ripley, A. Bronson Alcott, and Frances Parker wrote about and advocated for school reform that would feature holistic components in the American educational curriculum. The most successful of these men to impact mainstream education was Frances Parker, who went to Europe to study the ideas of Pestalozzi and Froebel. Unlike other Americans listed here whose work took place in private schools, Parker's efforts took place in public schools where he served as a superintendent after a long teaching career.

Maria Montessori, an Italian, was educated in medical science and approached learning from a scientific developmental perspective. Her work, based on scientific principles, became more influential than her predecessors', and today there are Montessori schools all over the world, with more than 3,000 in America alone. Montessori believed that children would naturally select what they wanted to learn and that a teacher's task was to create an inviting environment that provided choice—but choices that would promote and develop age-appropriate learning experiences. In a Montessori school, children are encouraged to learn at their own pace and to engage in self-selected learning activities.

In 1919, the owner of the Waldorf cigarette factory in Stuttgart, Germany, asked Rudolf Steiner to create a new school that would contrast mainstream education of the day. Steiner, a well-known writer and philosopher of that time, had already started a movement called Anthroposophy that he defined as "the wisdom of the human being." He believed in reincarnation and thought of education as one means through which we may develop our spirit as it progresses in this life and into the next. Humans, he suggested, are engaged in lifelong learning, primarily as an advancement of their spiritual being. Therefore, everything we do in life automatically has a spiritual element in it. Steiner's "Waldorf School" became very successful, and today there are "approximately 750 schools in 44 countries around the world" (Rocha, 2003, p. 77).

The Waldorf approach starts with Steiner's specific ideas regarding spirituality, developmental stages, and the purpose of life on earth. It is not a system that adheres to any particular religious dogma. The curriculum moves in blocks that correspond to the developmental stages of learners and it is highly stylized to take advantage of the philosophical ideas of Steiner. At least 2 years of specialized training at a Waldorf teachers school is required for certification as a Waldorf teacher and, beyond training, teachers are expected to be committed to their own spiritual and professional development. While Waldorf teachers have quite a lot of autonomy, their pedagogical choices must conform to the Waldorf frame and be structured around Steiner's developmental stages and what those imply.

Steiner created an approach that takes advantage of the learning abilities inherent in the three developmental stages he saw; it aims at teaching to the whole child rather than just to the intellect. Steiner believed that developmental stages shift every 7 years. During the first stage, the child is thought to be adjusting to the physical body and the physical nature of life. From ages 7 through 14 the child needs to focus on the "feeling life" and on imagination. The third stage, 14–21, focuses on intellectual development.

Following these stages, children in Stage 1 are presented with a curriculum that features a lot of physical learning through the arts, such as drawing, music, dance, and drama. It is believed that children learn best in the morning, so a specific rhythm that draws on this inclination is an important part of the curriculum. Games and physical activity are connected to subject matter whenever possible. Eurythmy, "music and speech expressed in bodily movement" (Rocha, 2003, p. 88), is an important element in a Waldorf school. Waldorf teachers receive special training in eurythmy and use it to enhance learning. Children in Stage 2 experience opportunities to develop perception, creativity, music, and feelings. It is the stage where feeling and intellect begin to become distinct, but it is not yet a time for intellect to be the focus. Stage 3 provides opportunities to develop intellect and to utilize all that has been carried forward from Stages 1 and 2.

The *Sudbury Valley School* was the first holistic school to ever be fully accredited. It opened in 1968 in Framingham, Massachusetts. Since then, the Sudbury School Network has evolved, with schools across the United States.

Sudbury schools are founded on democratic principles and the idea that children learn what they need when they need it. Students and faculty govern the school through decisions made in "meetings" wherein each participant has an equal vote. Classes, like those in mainstream schools, do not exist. Instead, students who are interested in a particular subject approach a faculty member and ask for help in the learning process. The teacher and student(s) enter into a contract once they reach an agreement about curriculum, goals, and time schedules. Children are never "assigned" material they do not ask for. Both academic and nonacademic subjects are available. For example, a learner may spend 3 months in woodworking or cooking, and then switch to math or reading. Daniel Greenberg's *Free at Last: The Sudbury Valley School* (1987) provides an enjoyable and thorough overview of the school and its principles.

Borrowing from various philosophical tenets found in Waldorf, Sudbury, or Montessori schools, other innovative or alternative schools and learning communities now offer parents and learners choices that go beyond the mainstream approaches found in public schools. The home-school movement has also gained strength and today more children are home-schooled in the United States than ever before. *Creating Learning Communities: Models, Resources, and New Ways of Thinking About Teaching and Learning* (R. Miller, 2000) is an excellent source to use as a starting place for learning about these alternative choices.

Philip S. Gang saw connections between Montessori principles and holistic worldviews. He coined the term *holistic education* and since the mid-1980s has been the leading advocate for the holistic education movement around the world. Gang believed that education should:

> Give young people a *Vision of the Universe* in which all animate and inanimate beings are interconnected and unified.
> Help students synthesize learning and discover the *interrelatedness of all disciplines*.
> Prepare students for life in the new age by emphasizing a *Global Perspective* and common human interests.
> Enable the young to develop a sense of harmony and *Spirituality*—which are needed to construct world peace (as cited in R. Miller, 1997, pp. 205–206).

In 1991 at the Global Alliance for Transforming Education (GATE) conference, directed by Gang, a position paper written by Ron Miller placed holistic education in a cultural context, and expanding on Gang's ideas, introduced 10 principles of holistic education that were endorsed by the conference attendees. These educators stated:

1. We assert that the primary—indeed the fundamental—purpose of education is to nourish the inherent possibilities of human development.
2. We call for each learner—young and old—to be recognized as unique and valuable.... Each individual is inherently creative, has unique physical, emotional, intellectual, and spiritual needs and abilities, and possesses an unlimited capacity to learn.
3. We affirm what the most perceptive educators have argued for centuries: education is a matter of experience. Learning is an active multi-sensory engagement between an individual and the world.
4. We call for wholeness in the educational process, and for the transformation of educational institutions and policies required to attain this aim. Wholeness implies that each academic discipline provides merely a different perspective on the rich, complex, integrated phenomenon of life.

5. We hold . . . that educators ought to be facilitators of learning, which is an organic, natural process and not a product that can be turned out on demand.
6. We call for meaningful opportunities for real choice at every stage of the learning process.
7. We call for a truly democratic model of education to empower all citizens to participate in meaningful ways in the life of the community and the planet.
8. We believe that each of us—whether we realize it or not—is a global citizen. . . . We believe that it is time for education to nurture an appreciation for the magnificent diversity of human experience.
9. We believe that education must spring organically from a profound reverence for life in all its forms. We must rekindle a relationship between the human and natural world that is nurturing, not exploitive.
10. The most important, most valuable part of the person is his or her inner, subjective life—the self or the soul. . . . We believe that education must nourish the healthy growth of the spiritual life, not do violence to it through constant evaluation and competition (as cited in R. Miller, 1997, p. 205).

Adding to the direction provided by GATE, the Holistic and Aesthetic Education Graduate Focus at the Ontario Institute for Studies in Education at the University of Toronto, has held four international conferences on holistic education. The fifth is scheduled for October 2007. *Holistic Learning and Spirituality in Education*, a collection edited by John P. Miller et al., features the work of selected conference presenters from the first three. This collection, perhaps more than any other, establishes holistic education as a wise and spiritual approach to learning.

A BRIEF CHRONOLOGY

1762 Jean-Jacques Rousseau argues that education should seek a connection between the "organic needs of human development and the rational requirements of the 'social contract'" (R. Miller, 1997, p. 92).

1809 Johann Heinrich Pestalozzi further develops Rousseau's theory. He used working farms as schools for students, mainly orphans, and taught them that "God's nature which is in you is held sacred in this House. We do not hem it in; we try to develop it. Nor do we impose on you our own natures . . . Under our guidance you should become men such as your natures—the divine and sacred in your nature—require you to be" (R. Miller, 1997, p. 98).

1826 Friedrich Froebel writes *The Education of Man*, after working for a few years with Pestalozzi. In this book he comes up with three central holistic themes: (1) Every person has the ability to unfold divinely; (2) The divine unfolding comes from a spontaneous creative nature in people; and (3) The educational environment should respect the fullness and natural stages of this unfolding (R. Miller, 1997, pp. 99–100). Froebel is best remembered for creating the kindergarten.

1830 The New England Transcendentalism movement begins. This movement addressed issues of religion, philosophy, politics, education, and social improvements. Many of the most influential thinkers in transcendentalism promoted a holistic approach to living.

1834 A. Bronson Alcott starts a school in the Masonic temple: the Temple School. He worked with William E. Channing and was a radical Transcendentalist. He hated materialism and believed that education must "nurture the full development of the human powers of each child" (R. Miller, 1997, p. 114).

1837 Henry David Thoreau studied with Emerson. He taught for a brief time but left it to live at Walden Pond. While he wrote on many philosophical topics, within education, he thought that the teacher should find as much to learn from the student as the student has to learn from the teacher. This idea is a central concern in holistic education.

1839 William E Channing, "The Great Awakener," a preacher for the Unitarian movement, writes that education starts with the child's nature and not the educators' preconceptions. Like Froebel, Pestalozzi, and Rousseau, he believed in the divine awakening within people, especially children.

1840 The American industrial revolution begins, which spurs the Civil War and end of slavery. This change also brought on many new radical thinkers and ideas.

1850 Ralph Waldo Emerson, a major figure of Transcendentalism, says, "The secret of education lies in respecting the pupil. It is not for you to choose what he shall know, what he shall do. It is chosen and foreordained, and he only holds the key to his own secret" (R. Miller, 1997, p. 108).

1861 Rudolph Steiner is born. He was an Austrian educator who wrote many books on philosophy, economics, education, and social conditions. He later founded the Waldorf Schools.

1870 Maria Montessori is born. She was a premier leader of holistic alternative education. Montessori was the first Italian woman to enter into medical school. She began working with disabled children, whether they be mentally retarded or with learning disabilities, and with these children she discovered new ways to teach and enhance learning abilities.

1894 Francis W. Parker, a public school educator, brings significant attention to holistic methods with his *Talks on Pedagogies*, which focused on the dignity of human nature.

1901 Francisco Ferrer, a radical anarchist, starts a school in Barcelona, the "Modern School." He was deeply influenced by Rousseau, Tolstoy, and the British anarchist William Godwin.

1907 Maria Montessori begins her educational theory work with children in slum areas. She believed that the spiritual development of children was as important as the learning of books.

1910 The Francisco Ferrer Association is founded.

1913 Steiner starts his own movement, "Anthroposophy." A core idea in anthroposophy is that "the inner life of humans, the soul, contains the deepest truths of human existence" (R. Miller, 1997, p. 169).

1919 The first Waldorf School is founded by Steiner.

1921 The Summerhill School is founded by A. S. Neill in England

1968 The first Sudbury School is opened.

1969 The Albany Free School opens in Albany, New York.

1970 The Open Classroom movement becomes controversial. The open classroom provides teachers, parents, and students with an equal voice in the participation in and administration of school affairs.

1971 Jean Piaget's theory of child development gets widely discussed.

1972 The Free School movement is developed. More people are looking at alternative ways to educate, reasons for dropping out of schools, and forming "free schools" or "open schools."

Mid-1980s Steiner's Anthroposophy Society is extended to Japan. Fifty-eight books by Japanese authors are published on Waldorf Education.

1980s The term *holistic education* is presented systematically, but independently, by American educator Ron Miller and by Canadian educator John P. Miller.

1988 The inaugural edition of *Holistic Educational Review (HER)* is issued.

1988 Edward T. Clark Jr. writes a seminal article in the *HER* titled "The Search for a New Educational Paradigm." This article approaches new ways of managing and structuring schools, teaching, and learning.

1990 The Chicago Statement on Education comes out of a retreat of 80 holistic educators.

1990 The Global Alliance for Transforming Education (GATE) conference is directed by Philip Gang. Several conferences are held in the next few years.

1991 GATE releases a position paper titled "Education 2000: A Holistic Perspective."

1996 John P. Miller's book *The Holistic Curriculum* is published.

1997 Twenty educators meet at the University of Nottingham in the United Kingdom for 2 days of seminars on the future of education and its evolution. The conference is known as the Nottingham Conference for Education in 2020.

1997 The first conference on holistic education is held at the Ontario Institute for Studies in Education (OISE) at the University of Toronto, titled "International Holistic Education Conference: Breaking New Ground." This conference is held every 2 years.

2000 Over a million families in the United States now homeschool their children.

2002 The ministry of education in Japan includes new aspects into their education. The three key words in this new aspect are "*kokoro-nokyoiku* (education for the heart and soul), *sogogakushyu* (integrated learning), and *tokushyoku, koseika* (the uniqueness of each school as well as of the individual person)" (J. P. Miller, 2005, pp.130–131).

2005 *Holistic Learning and Spirituality in Education*, edited by John P. Miller, Selia Karsten, Diana Denton, Deborah Orr, and Isabella Colalillo Kate, is published. It features presentations from three international holistic education conferences, "Breaking New Ground."

REFERENCES

Foehr, R. P., & Schiller, S. A. (Eds.). (1997). *The spiritual side of writing: Releasing the learner's whole potential.* Portsmouth, NH: Heinemann/Boynton Cook.

Greenberg, D. (1987). *Free at last: The Sudbury Valley School.* Framingham, MA: Sudbury Valley School Press.

Kane, J. (2000). Waldorf education: Reflections on the essentials. In John (Jack) P. Miller & Y. Nakagawa (Eds.), *Education and the soul.* Albany: State University of New York Press.

Kessler, R. (2000). *The soul of education.* Alexandria, VA: Association for Supervision and Curriculum Development.

Lantieri, L. (Ed.). (2001). *Schools with spirit: Nurturing the inner lives of children and teachers.* Boston: Beacon.

Miller, J. P. (1993). *Holistic teacher.* Toronto: OISE Press.

Miller, J. P. (1996). *The holistic curriculum* (rev. ed.). Toronto: OISE Press.

Miller, J. P. (2000). *Education and the soul: Toward a spiritual curriculum.* Albany: State University of New York Press.

Miller, J. P., Karsten, S., Denton, D., Orr, D., & Colalillo Kates, I. (Eds.). (2005). *Holistic learning and spirituality in education: Breaking new ground.* Albany: State University of New York Press.

Miller, R. (1991). *New directions in education: Selections from holistic review.* Brandon, VT: Holistic Education Press.

Miller, R. (1997). *What are schools for? Holistic education in American culture* (3rd ed.). Brandon, VT: Holistic Education Press.

Miller, R. (Ed.). (2000). *Creating learning communities: Models, resources, and new ways of thinking about teaching and learning.* Brandon, VT: The Foundation for Educational Renewal.

Palmer, P. J. (1998). *The courage to teach: Exploring the inner landscape of a teacher's life.* San Francisco: Jossey-Bass.

Rocha, D. L. D. (2003). *Schools where children matter: Exploring educational alternatives.* Brandon, VT: The Foundation for Educational Renewal.

CHAPTER 2

Creativity: A Holistic Route to Writing

Mainstream writing programs in institutions of higher education across the United States are generated by a long tradition of separating creativity from logical ways of knowing. In composition courses, academic discourse[1] dominates the curriculum even though it is only one rhetorical form. Indeed, most writing programs are built around the goal of competency in it.

In large state colleges and universities, English departments routinely offer 50 to 100 or more sections of freshman composition compared to one freshman-level creative writing course. Students are required to take one, two, and sometimes three courses of composition, while creative writing courses generally only fulfill electives. Unfortunately, the majority of students *never* study creative writing. In fact, creativity is rarely taught or promoted and may even be penalized in composition programs. An intense and provocative dichotomy between creativity and logical ways of knowing is sustained, and it permeates education to such a degree that when it is questioned, is done so in an environment of suspicion and stigma.

Within this system, almost all students learn to place a higher value on research than on creativity or on professions within the arts such as dance, music, or drama. Western cultures tend to perceive careers in artistic fields as those that are less financially stable than, for example, a career in law, medicine, or business, choices that typically rely on linguistics and logic as the primary way of knowing. Students learn to rely on analysis and argumentation. Analysis and argumentation are rhetorical acts wherein the parts are separated from the whole for closer scrutiny of their solitary function within the whole, not for their interconnections with other parts. In analysis, the sum of the parts equal the total of the whole.

Moreover, this view (and practice) of analysis contains a reductionist quality that weakens the act of knowing. This quality is too restrictive and causes writing to become an arduous time-intensive task that allows little room for original thought or creativity, especially when it becomes the primary element or preferred model for knowing. It is not holistic because it relies on logical and linguistic ways of knowing, and features disconnections rather than interconnections.

Analysis or argumentation from a holistic perspective sees the sum of the parts as greater than the total of the whole. In fact, the whole cannot be completely understood solely by investigating the parts; we must also review and understand the connections within the parts, the connections within the whole, and the connections to the exterior elements surrounding the whole. The connections and inclusion of the exterior elements enrich the phenomenon and enliven knowledge making.

Within mainstream education, but differing from composition programs, creative writing programs move beyond the logical and linguistic ways of knowing to include and connect with creative processes of the writers. As students discover their own creative processes, they learn that the act of creativity *refreshes their soul and then ignites cognition*; objective data simply function to support and supplement the creative impulse. They learn to value creativity as highly as, or even more highly than, logical and linguistic ways of knowing. As a result, students inculcate a reliance and dependence *on their ability to be creative*, and the creative process becomes *a routine, natural way of learning*. This is a holistic way of learning that balances multiple intelligences; it includes a broader field of rhetorical and social choices, and it connects writers to them.

Unfortunately, within mainstream education today, information, logic, and persuasion—the essential modes in research—still receive more value than creativity despite the work in multiple ways of knowing documented by Howard Gardner. Although Gardner's seven types of intelligence, "linguistic, logical mathematical, spatial, musical, kinesthetic, interpersonal, and intrapersonal" (as cited in J. P. Miller, 1993, p. 20), has received general acceptance,[2] mainstream education still relies primarily on linguistic and logical mathematical ways of knowing (Noddings, 1992, p. 31). This seems to be most unwise, considering what we know about creativity. We need to move closer to a holistic form of education—one that values creativity, rather than analysis, as the primary learning strategy—and one that is made available to large numbers of students, particularly students of writing.

Modifications to existing writing programs that would transform the logical and linguistic basis to one that is more holistic is not necessarily a difficult thing to do if we focus on the use of creativity as the primary learning strategy. We do not need to cut or replace composition courses with creative writing courses; we need to *redesign* composition courses so that creativity can *dominate* the curriculum in a way that also invites objective data to function in a *supportive* role. First, a working definition of creativity should inform and frame the new design, and second, the creative process(es) should be identified so that writers have a clear behavioral model to inform their decisions.

Activity in the field of creativity studies (what it is and how it works) has increased over the last 70 years, and is usually dominated by psychology. Social, psychological, emotional, cultural, and biological factors are most often featured. Studies tend to fall into two categories: idiographic research that relies on individual case studies, and nomothetic research that seeks discovery of general or universal laws that can be applied to all (Gardner, 1994, p. 143).[3]

Howard Gardner's writing, attempting to construct a bridge that spans idiographic and nomothetic research, presents a more holistic perspective, although he fails to account for the spiritual side of knowing. He stresses cognitive and developmental psychological frames that take into account social and motivational aspects of creativity. His approach is "inherently interdisciplinary" (1994, p. 145)—a feature that leans into holism. About his definition and approach, Gardner says:

1. I focus equally on problem solving, problem finding, and the creation of products, such as scientific theories, works of art, or the building of institutions.
2. I emphasize that all creative work occurs in one or more domains.[4] Individuals are not creative (or noncreative) in general; they are creative in particular domains of accomplishment and require the achievement of expertise in these domains before they can execute significant creative work.
3. No person, act, or product is creative or noncreative in itself. Judgments of creativity are inherently communal, relying heavily on individuals expert within a domain. (1994, p. 145)

Gardner's view requires a broadening of perspective that lets us see that "creativity emerges in virtue of a dialectical process among *individuals* of talent, *domains* of knowledge and practices, and *fields* of knowledgeable judges" (1994, p. 146). His work further relies on two general positions: one, that people can develop all seven intelligences he has already identified, and two, that creative people "are characterized particularly by a tension, or lack of fit, between the elements involved in a productive work" (1994, p. 146). He labels this tension *fruitful asynchrony*, and says that it is "the conquering of these asynchronies that leads to the establishment of work that comes to be cherished" (1994, p. 146).[5] In other words, fruitful asynchrony provides the initiating impulse for creativity. What does this mean for people who seek to produce a piece of writing? Let's move through Gardner's three phases of creativity to see.

First, writing can be identified as problem solving, and/or the creation of a product (the written document). The beginning step is to decide which one or if both task descriptors apply.

Second, the domain, or set of practices one needs, should be identified. Then the writer can determine whether or not their expertise is sufficient or if it needs development before the creative work is manifested. In many instances, actions taken to manifest the creative work increases the level of expertise and these actions may be self-motivated by the creator or externally motivated by an expert in the domain.

Third, since judgments of creativity are inherently communal, writers need connections with experts within the domain who can articulate previously set standards for determining the emergence of creativity. Standards might also serve to direct the creative action. For some people, standards might actually inhibit creativity if the person cannot imagine meeting or surpassing them. For other people, the standards may appear too limited and too easy to meet or surpass. In this case, the standards might initiate a new level of achievement, but if the achievement is too extreme to the community of judges a different type of tension can arise. The cliché often applied to such people is that they are "ahead of their time." Yet, many of our greatest thinkers and creators have been labeled as such and have depended on their own standards; they become their own judges and work to please their own innate need to create something new.

It is easy to see that fruitful asynchrony can begin in all three categories and that no person, act, or product is creative or noncreative in itself. Since elements in the creative act are interconnected, holism is strong. Moreover, the creative act in all of the three categories requires the writer to *imagine* that they can accomplish something new.

At the root of *imagine* is *image*. According to the research completed on imagery and creativity by Ainsworth-Land, the relationship between creativity and imagery is developmental. People can identify and use a creative process:

1. The first impulse is sense related and arises out of a physical need.
2. The second involves improvement of an idea or artistic product through analysis and evaluation.

3. The third requires synthesis, not just revision or modification. Something new or novel must be discovered through the synthesis before there is a breakthrough to new knowledge or understanding.
4. The final step, Ainsworth-Land states, occurs when "one's whole being comes into play with the conscious and unconscious minds, reason and intuition, inner and outer, subsumed into a kind of meta-consciousness. . . . The self is part of a larger reality. [Here, one is] building new perceptual order" (as cited in J. P. Miller, 1996, p. 94). This holistic process casts creativity as a self-motivated action that connects the individual inner life of the creator with the exterior social and environmental exigencies described so thoroughly by Gardner. Both Gardner and Ainsworth-Land provide models that can help us understand and implement creativity as the primary and dominant strategy for writing, regardless of any specific rhetorical genre we seek to produce.

The process described by Ainsworth-Land *naturally* activates learning, and with creativity as the dominant strategy, students awaken to the innate and universal human desire for learning. When students complete a creative project, they naturally combine analytic thinking, critical thinking, research, creativity, and reflection. They must imagine their project completed and then attempt to reach the image they have mentally created. As they reach toward completion, they participate physically and socially when choosing collaboration with peers and then again during the presentations of their completed projects.

Their intellect and spirit are awakened by work they choose, create, and design, and their intellectual abilities are stretched with the challenge of synthesizing material into a creative artifact that they judge to be aesthetically pleasing. A transcendent unity occurs when, through the creative impulse, these parts of the learner are integrated and harmonized within their expressive project.

Through creativity students further develop a holistic worldview—one that provides "an ability to see connections between diverse things and see the bigger picture" (Zohar & Marshall, as cited in Lantieri, 2001, p. 17). Students also have an opportunity to develop spiritual intelligence,[6] which Danah Zohar and Ian Marshall define as "intelligence with which we address and solve problems of meaning and value, the intelligence with which we can place our actions and our lives in a wider, richer meaning-giving context. It is the intelligence with which we can assess that one course of action or one life path is more meaningful than another" (as cited in Lantieri, 2001, p. 18). Zohar and Marshall "call spiritual intelligence the ultimate intelligence because it is the necessary foundation for the effective functioning of the other intelligences and because it has a transformative power" (as cited in Lantieri, 2001, p. 18).

The separation of church and state is a highly regarded mandate that most mainstream public schools maintain. Holistic educators seek the same goal and offer multiple definitions for secular spiritual approaches to education. For example, Linda Lantieri (2001) says, "Spiritual experience can be described as the conscious recognition of a connection that goes beyond our own minds or emotions," and spiritual approaches are "the kinds of approaches that encourage a commitment to matters of the heart and spirit that are among the positive building blocks of healthy development" (p. 16). Parker Palmer (as cited in Lantieri, 2001) tells us the spiritual voice is "the voice of the soul, that sacred place in every human being where suffering is transformed into creativity and from which generosity can flow" (p. 132). John P. Miller (1996) writes in *The Holistic Curriculum* that spirituality is the "sense of awe and reverence for life that arises from our relatedness to something both wonderful and mysterious" (p. 2). This is similar to Ron Miller's (2000) statement that spirituality is "some even larger dimension of cosmic purpose, which many people term as the 'spiritual' dimension" (p. 11).

My own definition is not so different from these. I believe a spiritual pedagogy is founded upon and develops our wonder and awe of the infinite mystery of the cosmos, of all people and gifts of the

Earth, and of our mental, physical, emotional, and creative abilities. From just these few working definitions we can see that spirituality is easily identifiable outside of religion; it is a flexible and varied topic that can sustain and enrich education.

Creativity as a dominant learning strategy fosters an environment where the "basic [human] need to create" (Gifford, 1956, p. 32) can thrive. Creativity also facilitates a spiritual approach to learning because creativity requires the learner to connect their inner being, their soul, to their exterior world. It asks that they find meaning and purpose in what they do—it evokes holism.

REFERENCES

Amabile, T. M. (1983). *The social psychology of creativity*. New York: Springer-Verlag.
Boden, M. A. (Ed.). (1994). *Dimensions of creativity*. Cambridge, MA: MIT Press.
Gardner, H. (1994). The creators' patterns. In M. A. Boden (Ed.), *Dimensions of creativity* (pp. 143–158). Cambridge, MA: MIT Press.
Gifford, D. (1956, October). *The creative process in the classroom*. Paper presented at the Conference on Creativity as a Process, Arden House, Harriman, New York.
Lantieri, L. (Ed.). (2001). *Schools with spirit: Nurturing the inner lives of children and teachers*. Boston: Beacon.
Michalko, M. (2001). *Cracking creativity: The secrets of creative genius*. Berkeley, CA: Ten Speed.
Miller, J. P. (1996). *The holistic curriculum*. Toronto: OISE Press.
Noddings, N. (1992). *The challenge to care in schools: An alternative approach to education*. New York: Teachers College Press.

NOTES

1. Academic discourse usually refers to writing that takes the forms of argumentation, objective data reporting, and research-based prose. A formal third-person voice is almost always used. Subjective and/or emotional content such as anecdotes or personal opinions are not permitted.

2. Gardner's work helped open doors for others to later research and identify emotional intelligence and spiritual intelligence.

3. For a fuller view of creativity studies than this space allows, see *Dimensions of Creativity*, edited by M. A. Boden, 1994, Cambridge, MA: MIT Press.

4. "A domain is a set of practices associated with an area of knowledge; the field consists of the individuals and institutions that render judgments about work in a domain" (Gardner, 1994, p. 152).

5. In this study, Gardner goes on to use even well-known creators: Sigmund Freud, Albert Einstein, Pablo Picasso, Igor Stravinsky, T. S. Eliot, Martha Graham, and Mahatma Gandhi—each exemplifying at least one of the seven intelligences Gardner identifies.

6. Gardner's intelligences, developed within cognitive psychology, do not include spiritual intelligence. Within the field of holistic education, however, spiritual intelligence is essential. Without the spiritual core, there is no holism.

CHAPTER 3

Contemplating Great Things in Soul and Place

Overview: Participants view photographs of beautiful places, write a reflective response, and share it with others. A process using movement to and from inner and exterior spaces and silence creates an atmosphere that encourages analysis, reflection, and creativity.
Materials: Photographs or postcards of beautiful places, paper or journal notebook, something to write with
Suggested Time: 90 minutes minimum, can be extended
Participants: At least two people are needed for this activity.
Types of Learning: Visual, verbal (written and spoken), physical, intellectual, emotional, spiritual, social, environmental, and reflective
Rhetorical Forms: Prose and poetry
Prerequisite: Knowledge of poetic forms (optional)

FOREWORD

This holistic writing activity allows people to create a poem, write a reflective response, and share it with others. It strengthens relationships with soil, soul, and society. At its core we find the soul; we find transformation as an ontological phenomenon of infinite capacity. This phenomenon can open us to the power we hold within to shape and live our lives. We learn to see that the inner and outer rhythms that shape life can be used for our benefit and growth. More important, we also learn that, once demystified, the transformative power of the soul can be accessible to us whenever we need it. We can understand, and share, the transformative power of the soul as a skill to use when we shape relationships with one another and with our world.

The activity below integrates mind, body, and soul in a process of harmonious interconnections between images, words, silence, and creativity. Images, words, and silence are used repeatedly to initiate a movement from outer to inner spaces and back again. This "is a basic human rhythm" (Neville, as cited in Kessler, 2000, p. 56) that I also consider as a practical gateway leading to creativity and transformation.

Participants are asked to express the inner rhythm by creating their own poem about the greatness they have been able to newly see. Kessler (2000) informs us that "when creativity breaks through . . . [m]ind, body, heart and spirit come together to spark the passion that fuels the motivation to learn to contribute and to savor our infinite capacity for growth" (p. 114). When people share their creations at the end of the writing process, the capacity for growth is proclaimed and witnessed within the community. This validates their soul. In this context, *soul* refers to the inner depths from which feeling, knowledge, and change originate.

This process further creates the potential for participants to understand that greatness is accessible to us at any time if we allow the soul to transform our vision and to see that great things help our souls to emerge. While the outer shell of the process is linear, activities within each step are not; they awaken the participants to infinite opportunities for seeing the greatness in soul and place. The relationship between linear and nonlinear ways of learning is created and allowed to flow. Ultimately participants learn that greatness is everywhere if we just let our souls feel and see it, and that the soul itself is a transformative power that we can access to resee the world.

Balance, inclusion, and connection—so vital to holistic learning (Miller, 1996, p. 3)—are maintained as they lead us to see that the transformative power of the soul can be studied as a phenomenon. As a phenomenon, this power can be sought; it does not need to remain a mystery. Our soul, then, becomes a paramount and practical place of growth of infinite learning.

THE ACTIVITY

Step 1: 2–5 minutes of contemplating place as depicted in photos of Austria, the Czech Republic, and Hungary (poetic image)
Step 2: 5–10 minutes of silent meditation (reverie and imagination)
Step 3: 5–10 minutes of journal writing on the greatness within these images of place (linguistic experience: connecting soul to place, combining mind and soul)
Step 4: 5 minutes of scrutiny of potential greatness in the place where the workshop is held (poetic image)
Step 5: 5–10 minutes of silent meditation (reverie and imagination)
Step 6: 5–10 minutes of journal writing on the greatness in the workshop place (linguistic experience: combining mind and soul)
Step 7: Time for writing a poem about place and self (creative, imaginative, imagistic, and linguistic experience)
Step 8: Discussion (linguistic connections to community: great things within and without)

In Step 1, photographs of indoor and outdoor European scenes offer a poetic image as a starting point for imagination. Although I find these foreign shots to be effective, primarily because they are unfamiliar and uncommon, any photograph of something beautiful or unfamiliar would work as well. These photos become the "poetic image" as Bachelard (1969) describes it, and they function as an externally located "great thing" that initiates the subsequent process. I ask students to contemplate the image and to imagine where the greatness exists in such a place.

The subsequent process combines imagination, the poetic image as great thing, and reverie about the great thing. Participants are led to transforming the way they view place and self and then ultimately to seeing the transforming power of the soul. They are transformed when they see that although the transforming power of the soul is primarily an internal event of viewpoint, it is also a phenomenon within them that they can call forth at will.

Silent meditation is a natural choice to enhance or deepen the quality of reverie. In the silent space of meditation, soul and mind can mingle; imagination can freely move in a state of reverie and without the restraints of order or structure. The reverie that Step 2 permits is natural and inevitable because, according to Bachelard, we cannot respond to the poetic image without a certain amount of reverie. For some people, particularly those who do not practice meditation, this activity can seem unfamiliar; 5 minutes of silent meditation feels extensive. Yet for those who do practice meditation, 5 minutes may feel insufficient. Regardless of previous experience, however, each participant is likely to experience "a rest for the nervous system, a respite from the demands of others, and a chance to visit one's own inner life" (Kessler, 2000, p. 38).

The journal writing in Step 3 returns the participants to prose, a linguistic activity that is familiar and offers a time for personal, yet private, expression. It brings participants back to the outer, and as such it offers a bit of pseudo-closure that is calming. It also extends the intellectual reflection on place and self. The calming effect of this familiar linguistic activity helps to ready participants for the next step, which can be quite disarming for a number of reasons depending on the immediate environment.

In Step 4, participants are asked to look for the greatness in the room they are in. As many of us know, classroom space can lack beauty. I generally find myself teaching in rooms made of painted beige cinderblock. Usually there is little daylight; shades are drawn and fluorescent lighting bears down unmercifully. Conference rooms are not much better either; chairs, tables, and perhaps audiovisual equipment is standard décor.

Creative tension arises when participants are asked to do something that at first seems illogical or impossible. Palmer (1998) says, "awareness is always heightened when we are caught in a creative tension" (p. 74). At first, participants react with surprise, thinking there is nothing great to be found in such space, but then their perception takes a noticeable shift.

As a facilitator for the process, I have been able to observe the way people suddenly acquire new vision when looking about the room. Some of them walk about to discover different vantage points. I have seen people touch and even smell wallpaper or painted walls. The more inquisitive might even crawl under a table and take a look from that point or sit on the floor instead of in a chair. This kind of exploration is encouraged by me. I often suggest using movement at this step in the activity as a means to see differently and as a means for knowing through the body. This step moves the participant into a deeper imaginative event that extends and further develops the potential for transformation.

Step 5 calls for additional reverie. It allows space for the imagination to again move toward transformation. The reverie in this step may actually be deeper because it may not feel as unfamiliar as it did earlier. Participants should be more relaxed at this stage. This is important because "when a relaxed spirit meditates and dreams [as we hope they are doing during this step], immensity seems to expect images of immensity. The mind sees and continues to see objects, while the spirit finds the nest of immensity in an object" (Bachelard, 1969, p. 190). As one might assume, it is especially helpful at this point to extend the time for silent meditation. Even with people new to meditation or silence, I try to allow the full 10 minutes. With more experienced participants, 15 minutes is even more desirable.

With this extended time, people are more likely to see the poetic image within the space around them *and* see that the soul shapes what we see. Bachelard says that "we are obliged to acknowledge that poetry is a commitment of the soul. A consciousness of the soul is more relaxed, less intentionalized than a consciousness associated with the phenomena of the mind" (1969, p. xvii). In a meditative silent state, when engaged with a poetic image, participants begin from a relaxed position and the mind is less restricted. The soul can rise up and emerge. Then, its ability to shape the way we view our world can be recognized.

At this point, participants should "realize within [themselves] the pure being of pure imagination" (1969, p. 184). They might also reach a more holistic view seeing that "the gifts of silence are intertwined; they cannot really be separated into cognitive, psychological, physiological, or spiritual" (Kessler, 2000, p. 43).

After the silent meditative reverie, participants are again asked to return to journal writing in Step 6. While it returns them to a familiar feeling and condition, it also is a prewriting activity for Step 7. It is a stress-free way of releasing insights and realizations experienced during Step 5. I don't allow too much time for this journal writing — 10 minutes at the most. Sometimes, though, people want more time for this. They seem to be flowing over with ideas and language and they want to let them out. I take this as evidence of what Palmer (1998) calls "the power of the living subject" (p. 103). He says that "when we make the subject the center of our attention, we give it the respect and authority that we normally give only to human beings. We give it ontological significance (p. 103).

Furthermore, Bachelard (1969) says, "The communicability of an unusual image is a fact of great ontological significance" (p. xiii). This ontological energy further primes them for creative expression in Step 7 because its dynamism can take shape in the poetic image. In this way, participants are dealing with the nature of being, reality, and ultimate substance.

Step 7 asks that participants write a poem about the greatness in place and self. By writing a poem, participants are taking space, their position in and view of it, and using it as an act of expansion. Bachelard (1969) states that "whatever affectivity that colors a given space, whether sad or ponderous, once it is poetically expressed, the sadness is diminished, the ponderousness lightened. Poetic space, because it is expressed, assumes values of expansion" (p. 201). Through creativity and expansion, participants experience a new awareness and open themselves to the transforming power of the soul. They learn, as Parker Palmer (1998) tells us, that great things "are the irreducible elements of life itself" (p. 109). They also learn that to see great things we must turn inward to the soul and let it guide our vision.

It is essential to allow sharing time to close the activity in Step 8. Facilitators can invite participants to read their poetry, share their emotions experienced throughout, ask questions, and/or give feedback or suggestions for changes in the process. The invitation must be sincere. Some people may not want to read their poem if it is too personal or if they just want to keep it private. Those who do want to share openly with the group do so with joy and excitement about the process. Their proclamations often encourage others to also share. More often than not, we have needed more time than I had scheduled for this part of the process. Yet, with just a little sharing, participants themselves validate creativity as a mode of knowing, and the phenomenon of transformation is manifested for everyone to see. It is demystified and appears as a normal and *accessible* function of soul.

To encourage nonjudgmental communication at this point, I sit quietly and let participants guide the conversation along lines they choose. I withhold opinions, but answer questions whenever asked. Most of the time, people are eager to read their poems, have interesting comments about their experiences throughout the whole process, and offer useful feedback about ways to alter the process. I can count on people to always share insight and growth, because they have reached a new awareness of their abilities to shape the world and understand the transformative power of soul in new ways.

VARIATIONS ON A THEME

Variations in this process are interesting to experiment with and have convinced me that the activity is extremely versatile and doesn't lose its transformative potential. For instance, weather permitting, the activity is especially potent for connecting to our Earth if participants can be taken out of doors and directed through the steps while sitting on the ground. Most recently, I inserted an additional step between Steps 6 and 7 when I asked students to pair off, hold both hands while gazing into each other's eyes and to simply look for the greatness in the other person. This variation elicited a stronger awareness of community and self. I have also asked participants to write letters (to their mother, friend, husband, significant other, or whomever they select) instead of a journal write or a poem. Rather than creating a poem, participants are sometimes directed to draw a picture or write a song.

I prefer to end with a creative act, because I believe creativity increases with practice and is directly connected to imagination. The imagination can lead us to break barriers, develop new consciousness, and to experience the highest intuitive knowing. In this state, we can then experience the unity of inner and outer spaces, seeing that all is interconnected. This activity can also become a delightful way of writing various poetic forms if those are introduced prior to the activity.

REFERENCES

Bachelard, G. (1969). *The poetics of space*. Boston: Beacon.
Kessler, R. (2000). *The soul of education*. Virginia: Association for Supervision and Curriculum Development.
Miller, J. P. (1996). *The holistic curriculum*. Toronto: OISE Press.
Palmer, P. J. (1998). *The courage to teach: Exploring the inner landscape of a teacher's life*. San Francisco: Jossey-Bass.

NOTE

A version of this chapter appears as an essay in *Holistic Learning and Spirituality in Education* by John P. Miller et al., 1996, Toronto: OISE Press.

CHAPTER 4

Walking in the Spirit of the Medicine Wheel: Learning to See What We Normally Do Not See

Overview: This activity contains five parts: Drawing the Medicine Wheel, Reflective Writing, Activating Volition for Promises of Future Action, Discovering Connections with Others, and Serving Others. Participants learn about the gifts of the four directions and move around a medicine wheel that they create.

Materials: Drawing paper; heavy cardboard such as poster board, wood slabs, or animal hide large enough for drawing the medicine wheel (I suggest starting with paper or poster board.); pencils, crayons, markers, and paint; something to use for creating a large circle (I've used pie tins, dinner plates, the rim of a round wastebasket.); a ruler or yardstick or anything that can be used to draw straight lines across the entire circle (If circles within the outer circle are desired, a compass is useful.)

Suggested Time: 2 hours and 10 minutes minimum. The times listed below are suggested times only, not requirements. This activity contains five detailed steps that could easily be extended over five separate sessions or more. If more extensive reflection or writing is desired, time may be extended. The medicine wheel may also be repeatedly used for infinite learning experiences and for creating many plans for promises of future action.

Types of Learning: Drawing, reflecting, analysis, writing, discussion. This activity moves beyond a strictly cognitive approach to learning and relies on the physical, emotional, mental, and spiritual ways we learn.

Participants: Small groups preferred. If doing this alone, skip Part 4 or modify it to attain feedback from people who have not completed the activity.

Rhetorical Forms: Self-selected by participant. The activity asks for writing at various spots. This writing could take the form of lists, sentences, songs, poems, essays, letters, and journal entries.

Prerequisite: None

INTRODUCTION

The medicine wheel is a Native American symbol representing all that has been made available to human beings as a journey of life that promotes the development of our hidden potentialities. It is a circle divided into four equal sections that symbolize the four directions: north, east, south, and west. The center, where all four directions are connected, symbolizes a person's volition, or will.

The lines in the medicine wheel usually are painted in four colors, white, black, yellow, and red, which represent the four races of people on the Earth. Again, at the center of the wheel, all are connected. The sections of the medicine wheel may also be seen as symbolic of the four dimensions of people: mental, spiritual, emotional, and physical. These are connected and developed through the use of our volition.

The four directions can also lead us to see the interconnections between the mineral, plant, animal, and human kingdoms in the universe (Bopp, Bopp, Brown, & Lane, 1984, pp. 29–32). When moving around the medicine wheel, we follow the natural rhythm of the Earth, beginning in the east.

The Medicine Wheel, as a path for life, is a journey that promises continuous growth throughout our lives. It also is based upon wholeness and interconnections between all things. It has a deeply spiritual quality to it, and it is also very practical and easy to integrate into daily living. On a spiritual level, the medicine wheel helps us see what we do not normally see. As we move from one direction to another and interconnections are revealed, we can learn about things in ourselves and in others. We can learn about the interconnectedness of all in the world. We can learn about our past, our present, and our future.

GIFTS FROM THE FOUR DIRECTIONS

East

The east is the place of new beginnings. Think of the sun that rises each morning. It brings light. It starts life afresh. Its light is gentle, guileless, and innocent. There is spontaneity, joy, and a sense of renewal at each dawn. It is easy to feel purity and hope. In the east we are able to love in a way that doesn't question others and doesn't call attention to itself. We have courage, truthfulness, and leadership as we guide others. We can experience beautiful speech even as we are vulnerable. We have the ability to see clearly and can focus, trusting in our own vision. We can stay tuned to the present time and concentrate with ease. The east helps us see things in perspective and lets us be devoted in our service to others. It is a place of birth and rebirth and it illuminates us with light (Bopp et al., 1984, p. 72).

South

The south is a place of fullness and summer light. It is kind, generous, and full of love. It is a place of strong growth where the senses are developed and where we are passionately involved with the world. We yearn to be with the one person we love. There is a youthful quality, and the heart is bursting with compassion as it is attracted to good and repulsed by bad, especially senseless violence. It is also a place where we find the ability to express our hurt and bad feelings as well as our joy and good feelings. We are able to set aside our strong feelings as we strive to serve others. We are able to appreciate and to express ourselves through music. It is a place of balance and development of the physical body even as our appetites are controlled. We set goals in the south and hold on to idealism (1984, p. 72).

West

We go inward for meditation, dreams, and deep inner thoughts when we enter the west. Although there is darkness, it is a darkness that lends itself to intuitive knowing and reflective thoughts. We test our will in the west as we struggle to assist other people and as we reach for inner vision of our potentialities and possibilities. Humility attaches itself to us and promotes our ability to make sacrifices. These lead us to a greater awareness of our spiritual qualities.

We also develop respect for our elders and for others' beliefs and their attempts to find spirituality. We enjoy silence, use silence to promote the gifts and lessons of the west, and we learn to enjoy being alone. We develop perseverance and determination to finish tasks. Ceremony, ritual, and spiritual practices such as fasting become attractive. We learn how to recognize and manage our personal power, which often leads to spiritual insight, clear self-knowledge, and a high moral code (1984, p. 73).

North

The north is a place of wisdom and maturity where tasks are completed and where we learn to live in moderation and with justice. We honor our elders, particularly for their wisdom and intellectual gifts such as thinking, analyzing, calculating and speculating, organizing, understanding, interpreting, and for their ability to see how all things fit together. We learn how to problem-solve, how to criticize, and how to discriminate in helpful ways. It is the place where we develop these same abilities that our elders demonstrate. We can develop detachment and find freedom from fear, hate, love, and even from knowledge. It is also where our intuition is made conscious and we sense how to live a balanced life. We gain confidence and an ability to make predictions and to live at the center of things (1984, p. 73).

THE ACTIVITY

The five parts below are designed to address a *generalized focus* on self and elements connected to the individual writer. However, this focus can be shifted to a *specific focus* on an idea, issue, or problem. To make such a shift, simply focus on the idea, issue, or problem in your mind as you complete the various steps. Let all you do pertain to that idea, issue, or problem. By doing this, the activities can be repeated all through the years of your life as a way to illuminate and discover what you have not yet seen.

Part 1: Drawing the Medicine Wheel (30 minutes)

1. Draw a rather large circle on the surface of your drawing material.
2. Draw two straight lines across the circle so that they dissect in the center.
3. If you want to depict the center where volition is found, you can draw a smaller circle or square around the center so that there is a circle within a circle or a square within the circle.
4. On a separate piece of paper, select gifts that appeal to you at the present time from each of the four directions.
5. For each gift, write a sentence or two that explains your choice
6. Next, at the end of each written explanation, draw a symbol that can depict that gift. For example, you might want to use a star to symbolize confidence or an arrow to depict freedom from fear. Maybe a scale would symbolize justice or a balanced life. Select symbols that feel right for you. Numbers might appeal to you, too. Seven becomes love, nine is justice, and so forth.
7. Pick a segment for each direction on the medicine wheel. Draw your symbols and place them in strategic spots. Let your intuition guide your placement. Don't think about it very hard or even at all. Just put them where you think they look good. Use color to enhance your choices and/or to emphasize the symbolic meaning.

Part 2: Reflective Writing (30 minutes)

1. Review the visual qualities of your entire medicine wheel and write a description of them. Explain what the symbols represent and give reasons for selecting that symbol. Begin in the east, move to the south, then the west, and finally to the north.
2. After writing about all four directions, draw conclusions about your current position in the world and how you are relating to the people, events, and places in your life at this time.
3. Draw conclusions about your soul, the society of which you are a part, and about your relationship to the Earth.
4. Try to identify the items that motivate you most strongly. Include a statement about where you would next like to go or in what area you would like your development to be focused.

Part 3: Activating Volition for Promises of Future Action (30 minutes)

Volition is the energy we use to motivate ourselves, whether that be making decisions or taking actions. It is placed at the center of the wheel because it connects the gifts from the four directions and is the primary force to use to develop these gifts. Volition can be exercised by activating five steps:

1. Giving attention (concentration)
2. Setting the goal
3. Initiating the action
4. Showing perseverance
5. Completing the action (Bopp et al., p. 14)

If there are more gifts at this time appearing in the east, it might be a time for you to make specific decisions or to take specific actions to further develop those gifts.

1. Look at what you have already written, select a single item that you would like to focus on and write a plan of action to develop it. Which direction does this item come from? Decide if you can use other gifts in that same direction to support this item. Also look at the other three directions to select gifts from them that complement your development of this item.
2. From the five steps above, select the appropriate ones to use as you plan to develop this item.
3. Write a plan of action for developing your growth with this item.
4. Write down what you expect to gain from developing this item.
5. To conclude, write about how this plan stimulates your soul, your place in society, and/or your relationship with the Earth.

Part 4: Discovering Connections With Others (30 minutes)

1. Pick two or three people to spend time with.
2. Display your medicine wheel to the group and read aloud your writing.
3. As you listen to others, write a list of items that are the same as yours.
4. When everyone has shared, before group discussion write a list of things you now see about your own plan that you didn't see before.
5. Finally discuss the plans for future growth and offer comments or suggestions for modifications. Record those that seem appealing for your use.

Part 5: Serving Others (10 minutes)

To conclude, write about how your plan serves your soul, your society, and/or the Earth. Decide where your plan mostly serves and imagine how it might be extended to serve more broadly.

REFERENCE

Bopp, J., Bopp, M., Brown, L., & Lane, P. (1984). *The sacred tree*. Alberta, Canada: Four Worlds Development Press.

CHAPTER 5

Write Your Own Ending

Overview: Participants read part of a play and then write their own ending for it. A group discussion featuring the new endings and comparing them to the original ending follow the writing. During the discussion, relevant topics from the play's content are explored.
Materials: Pen and paper
Suggested Time: One hour, minimum. This can easily be stretched out depending on variations writers or facilitators initiate.
Types of learning: Connecting art, history, social science, drama, and philosophy. Physical, emotional, mental, social, environmental, and spiritual. This activity can be used as a smaller part of a larger unit on drama[1] or used alone.
Participants: Small groups preferred
Rhetorical Forms: Drama
Prerequisite: Partial play reading
Facilitator Preparation: Play selection. For the sake of providing a specific context, the one-act, one-set play *K2* by Patrick Meyers has been selected. Another short story, novel, or play could be selected. *K2* is an extended argument between two friends who are mountain climbing. Caught in an avalanche at 27,000 feet, one man is injured, unable to descend or ascend. He argues for his friend to leave him knowing he will die. Does his friend leave or stay? If the friend stays, he too shall die. *K2* presents a situation in nature that demands an intense ethical decision regarding life and death. It raises philosophical questions about

faith, the role of friendship, duty to family, self-development choices, and responses to tragedy. It also demands that readers examine their attitudes toward nature, natural calamity, and the human role in nature.

The facilitator should read the literary selection first and decide how much writers should read before writing their own ending.

THE ACTIVITY

1. Writers should receive copies of the partial play and read it before completing the steps below.
2. In groups of two to four, writers can discuss how they would end the play.
3. Groups write their own ending.
4. After all the groups have written their ending, each group presents it to the others and gives reasons for its choices.
5. A general discussion regarding choices can guide the groups.
6. Groups are given the original ending to read.
7. A discussion on the play's original ending and on the differences presented by the various groups' endings and by rhetorical choices writers make when writing drama concludes the activity.

REFERENCE

Meyers, P. (2003). *K2*. In J. Stanford (Ed.), *Responding to literature: Stories, poems, plays and essays* (4th ed., pp. 891–913). Boston: McGraw-Hill.

NOTE

1. Write Your Own Ending was originally created by Clint Burhans to fulfill a requirement in English 460: Senior Seminar: Issues in English, at

Central Michigan University. In his project, this activity was presented as a small segment within a large multidisciplinary semester-long course aimed at adolescents attending Windsor House Alternative School in Vancouver, British Columbia, Canada. Students at this school are free to study what they wish when they wish. Clint's course used drama to unite the various disciplines he wanted to blend into a holistic learning experience. He asked students to write, produce, and perform their own play. *K2* and the Write Your Own Ending activity was an introduction to dramatic form, audience expectations, and how content can determine a writer's choices. He stated that he wanted students "to learn how drama is used to express thoughts and feelings about the world, and how they can find out about their own thoughts and feelings through the words and actions of others." When Clint facilitated this activity in the senior capstone presentation (a graduation requirement at CMU), the participants responded well to it and enjoyed a lively conversation about the ethical and environmental issues presented in *K2*. It was a highly successful presentation and was selected for the use in this book on those grounds. Clint was kind enough to grant permission for its use here.

CHAPTER 6

The Connected Self

Overview: Participants write a self-profile, a partner profile, or a combination of these after exploring holistic qualities (emotional, physical, intellectual, social, aesthetic [beauty], spiritual, universal) of their self and their partner. The writing process of drafting, writing, and revising is suggested. Writers also need to select an audience for their writing and specific rhetorical strategies to use when writing.

Materials: Freezer paper or drawing paper; crayons, markers, and colored pencils; any other art supplies desired; writing paper and pen

Suggested Time: Time can be determined by the writers and/or the facilitator. Time is needed for the following four steps:

1. Prewriting activities
2. The writing process
3. Reflective meta-writing
4. Celebrating the connected self

Types of Learning: Verbal, visual, mental, emotional, physical, spiritual, social
Participants: Partners
Rhetorical Forms: Biographical and autobiographical essay
Prerequisite: None

THE ACTIVITY

Part 1: Prewriting Activities

1. Each participant should fill out the form titled "Holistic Self Profile."
   a. Let intuition guide your response. Do not "think" about your response at all, just write down the first words that come to your mind.
2. Each participant should then draw a circle on the drawing paper provided, then in the circle draw an abstract image for each metaphor he or she wrote on this form.
3. Partnerships need to be formed next.
4. Partners should discuss each other's drawings, including any insights, surprises, or expectations they may have discovered in this process. On a separate piece of paper, jot down a few notes about these for use when you draft the essay.
5. Identify qualities you shared with each other during this process. Again, jot these down on a separate piece of paper.
6. Partners should fill out the form titled "Shared Qualities."
7. Partners then draw an oblong circle that can serve as a bridge or connector for each of their individual circles. They should then draw abstract symbols for the metaphors written on this form. Partners should end up with a visual that contains their two circles that are connected by the oblong bridge.

Part 2: The Writing Process

1. Participants need to decide whether they want to write alone or work collaboratively. If they decide to collaborate, they produce one essay only. If they decide to work alone, they still seek support and guidance from their partner during the writing process.

2. Writers select an audience for their essay and decide what information this audience finds most useful and why they might want to obtain it.
3. Writers select a rhetorical aim (persuasive, informative, or expressive; see Appendix B).
4. Partners select an appropriate organizational strategy to use when writing the essay. They might choose from classification, compare, contrast, narration, description, definition, process analysis or casual analysis, and illustration (see Appendix B). Using a combination of strategies is also an option. Writers should feel free to shift strategies as needed when writing the essay.
5. Title the essay "The Connected Self" and select a focus. Focus selection is somewhat directed by audience and aim. You may want to focus on:

    self-profile (autobiography)
    or partner profile (biography)
    or both (combining the above)

6. Write the first draft.
7. Review the first draft with your partner.
8. Make revision decisions.
9. Write the second draft.
10. Repeat the review and revision process as many times as you think necessary.
11. Reach a final draft.

Part 3: Reflective Meta-Writing

1. Attach a closing statement that lists the following elements in the final draft:

    a. Audience
    b. Aim

c. Focus
  d. Strengths
  e. What was omitted or changed from previous drafts
  f. What the writers like about their essay
  g. What the writers don't like about their essay
  h. A comment about prewriting activities that explains to what degree the activities were helpful.

Part 4: Celebrating the Connected Self

For Classroom Formats

The teacher or facilitator can initiate a group discussion that invites writers to

1. Share what they learned about themselves;
2. Share what they learned about their partner;
3. Discuss the prewriting activities;
4. Discuss the writing process;
5. Discuss their emotions about any of the above;
6. Suggest ways of improving the activities;
7. Suggest ways the prewriting activities might be used to generate other written genres, such as poetry or song lyrics; and
8. Give reasons they may or may not feel more connected to themselves or others in the class.

For Individual Writers

Writers might want to write a follow-up essay that features ideas suggested for writers in a classroom format. Or, they may want to have a conversation about their experiences with someone who is uninformed about the activities—perhaps a friend, parent, grandparent, sibling, neighbor, etc.

Holistic Profile

Instructions:

1. Fill in the blanks with single words or short phrases.
2. Don't take time to think about the words, just use the first word that comes to mind. Let your intuition guide you.
3. After filling out the chart, represent each word written with a symbolic image on drawing paper.

Aspects	Static (No change)	Dynamic (Changes)	Metaphoric (Symbolic comparison)
Emotional			
Physical			
Intellectual			
Social			
Beauty			
Spiritual			
Universal			

Shared Qualities

Instructions:

1. Fill in the blanks with single words or short phrases that are the same or are similar to those that appear on both Holistic Profiles.
2. Discuss the similarities *and* discuss those that were not included on the shared qualities form.

Aspects	*Static* (No change)	*Dynamic* (Changes)	*Metaphoric* (Symbolic comparison)
Emotional			
Physical			
Intellectual			
Social			
Beauty			
Spiritual			
Universal			

CHAPTER 7

Visioning in Silent Community

Overview: Participants read a short literary selection. (I have used selections from fiction, nonfiction prose, and poetry.) Each participant selects two or three key quotes that may represent the overall meaning in the literature. Then, with a partner and in silence, participants draw a nonrepresentational (abstract) image of meaning that corresponds to one selected passage. During this process, participants shall not write notes or use verbal language to communicate with their partner. After the drawing is completed, participants write a brief explanation of the image. The final stage is to form a "community collage" and discuss it as well as the process used to create it. The collage is a visual and tangible element; it melds the phenomenological variance that naturally and spiritually arises out of the silent space people use for creativity and literary visioning in silent community.

Materials: Markers, crayons, color pencils, poster board, writing paper, pens or pencils, scotch tape, scissors

Suggested Time: 60–90 minutes

Types of learning: Reading, drawing, writing, reflecting, discussing; physical, emotional, mental, verbal, visual, spatial, spiritual

Participants: Partners and whole class sizes, such as 25–30 people

Rhetorical Forms: Paragraphs and/or short essays

Prerequisite: Advanced reading ability

Preliminary Preparation for Facilitator:

1. On the reverse side of each poster board, draw a line that divides the poster board into two jigsaw puzzle shapes. Each part

of the first poster board is numbered 1, so you will have two 1s, two 2s, two 3s, and so on. Then cut the poster board into puzzle parts. You should end up with a collection of jigsaw pieces that can easily be reassembled later by simply looking for both 1s, 2s, 3s, and so on.
2. Select a short reading passage that can be read in about 5 minutes and make enough copies of it for all participants to use. Nonfiction, fiction, and poetry work well for this activity.
3. At the beginning, it is useful to emphasize that the silence in the activity facilitates the spiritual and practical use of silence and art as a means to interpret literary texts and to build classroom community. A preliminary statement to this effect invites the silence and contextualizes it to a point that people desire to cooperate. Silence is quite uncomfortable and difficult for some people to use. The context helps give those people a reason to persevere and to tolerate their discomfort if it should arise. It is also helpful to give people "permission" to silently leave the room if the silence is just too hard to accommodate.
4. Make enough copies of the instructions for each partnership to refer to during the time of silence. This helps if they should have questions.

THE ACTIVITY

1. The facilitator passes out copies of the literature and copies of the instructions.
2. This activity uses a lot of silence. Please hold all questions until the silence is broken at the end of the activity.
3. Pick a partner.
4. Select one passage or idea from the reading that seems important to both of you. Please do not talk. You may point to parts in the reading selection that you might want to consider.

5. After selecting the passage or idea, write it (exactly as it appears in the text) on the side of the poster board that is already numbered, and then write this passage on a separate piece of paper. This is used in a later step.
6. On the side of the poster board that is not numbered, create a colorful abstract image that reflects the meaning in the passage or idea you have selected. Please do not write notes or use verbal language to communicate with your partner. Try to use the entire surface of the poster board.
7. When you are finished drawing, write a brief explanation of your image on the piece of paper from Step 4. The facilitator collects these at the end of our discussion.
8. Give the drawing to the facilitator, who then builds a collage as people finish writing.
9. Finally, each participant should write a brief personal response to (a) silence, (b) their drawing, and (c) the group collage. The facilitator collects these after the discussion.
10. When you are finished writing, please put your pen down. After everyone is finished writing, we break silence and discuss our experiences.
11. If you are finished before other people, please do not break silence until the facilitator gives a signal.
12. Participate in a general whole-group discussion.

NOTE

This activity was presented at the International Holistic Education Conference: Breaking New Ground, Toronto, Canada, 2003.

CHAPTER 8

Screenplay Writing

Overview: Participants write a partial screenplay based on a short story. This provides opportunities for analysis of literary and cinematic elements that are needed during creative writing and during the adaptation process.

Materials: A collection of short stories, samples of professional screenplays, word-processing software, and computers

Optional Materials: Drawing paper and markers for creating storyboards, recording equipment for burning CDs or creating tapes, *The Elements of Writing About Literature and Film* by McMahan, Funk, and Day (1988)

Suggested Time: 36 hours minimum

Types of learning: Verbal, visual, mental, emotional, physical, spiritual, social

Participants: Writers might work alone, with a partner, or in groups of three or four. Groups larger than four generally have difficulty arranging writing time that suits all members.

Rhetorical Forms: Creative writing, literary analysis, reflective evaluations, informative prose

Prerequisite: Writers need to have completed reading a collection of short stories before beginning this activity. Writers need to be familiar with both literary and cinematic elements. See the attached list and see McMahan et al. (1988) for definitions or descriptions. Writers need to have discussed the factors that create the unique circumstances that govern literary writing and those that govern film making (in other words, why a book cannot be exactly like a film and a film cannot be exactly like a book).

THE ACTIVITY

1. After reading a collection of short stories, select a single story *or* a sequence of scenes from one story upon which to base your screenplay.
2. Decide how far you wish to "depart" from the original plot.
3. The final project should include in this order:
   a. A cover sheet with title and name(s)
   b. A brief analysis of the whole collection of short stories that describes strengths and weaknesses (This page documents that the whole book has been read and understood.)
   c. A list of literary elements used in the screenplay
   d. A list cinematic elements used in the screenplay
   e. A casting list, which names actors and actresses and describes a type of actor or actress
   f. A list of music selections (Optional: A CD or tape containing the music selections in the order as they appear in the screenplay. If one selection is used 3 times in the screenplay, it would also need to appear 3 times on the CD or tape.)
   g. The screenplay in screenplay format[1]
   h. A list of "departures" made from the story and the reasons they were made
   i. A self-evaluation of the work (If working in groups, there should be one evaluation for each group member, written by that person.)
   j. A group evaluation about ways the group worked together, if applicable (There should be one evaluation written by the group.)

LITERARY ELEMENTS

Character development
Protagonist
Antagonist
Foil

Stereotype
Dialogue
Plot
Theme
The classical dramatic structure
Symbolism
Motif
Point of view (There are four major types: omniscient, dramatic, limited, and unreliable.)
Dramatic irony
Hyperbole
Foreshadowing
Flashbacks
Chronological order
Allusion
Ambiguity
Coherence
Catharsis
Epiphany
Subplot
Metaphor
Simile
Setting
Mood

CINEMATIC ELEMENTS

In addition to the literary elements above, film can also contain the following:

Props
Crosscutting
Sequence
Casting
Music and/or sound
Lighting

Color
Over-the-shoulder shots
Extreme close-ups
Close-ups
Medium close-ups
Medium shots
Full shots
Long shots
Surveying pan
Two-shot, three-shot
Cut in
Cut away
Zoom in
Zoom out
Reaction shot
Fade ins
Fade outs
Dissolves
Cuts
Superimpositions
Wipes
Slit screens
Film and slides
Keys

REFERENCE

McMahan, E., Funk, R., & Day, S. (1988). *The elements of writing about literature and film.* New York: Macmillan.

NOTE

1. Screenplay format varies in form. I tell writers to create a consistent format of their own (e.g., all subheadings might be bold, dialogue centered, etc.).

CHAPTER 9

Info-Commercial

Overview: The info-commercial is a 15-minute mini-drama based on the classical dramatic structure (exposition, rising action, climax, falling action, denouement) that persuades the audience to read, or not to read, a particular novel, short story, poem, play, or essay. Participants are asked to include interconnections to soil, soul, and society.

Materials: Pen and paper, large sheets of construction paper, props (to be determined by the participants), Response Guides

Suggested Time: To be determined by number of participants. Time for outside planning is needed as is time for presenting the info-commercial. Time for reviewing Response Guides and for reflecting on ways to improve the info-commercial. Time for drafting a short essay that describes future improvements to the info-commercial.

Participants: Small groups are preferred, but partners or individuals could complete this activity.

Types of Learning: Visual, verbal (written and spoken), physical, intellectual, emotional, spiritual, social, environmental, and reflective

Rhetorical Forms: Persuasive drama and reflective, analytic prose

Prerequisite: Participants might select their own book or essay to base their info-commercial on or the facilitator could provide one. Each group should have a different title, so the facilitator needs to check on this if participant selection occurs.

Precautions: Prohibit violence or extreme sexual situations. Participants should be encouraged to use a style or approach that is safe, fun, and respectful rather than those that might be considered as X-rated or as sensationalized negativity.

THE ACTIVITY

Part 1

1. Form small groups.
2. Each group should select a novel, play, short story, poem, or essay to use for this activity and read it.

Part 2

1. List all the literary reasons that might convince someone to read this piece of literature. For example, maybe the writing style flows easily and is accessible, or perhaps the ideas are relevant to the audience members.
2. List all the literary reasons that might prevent someone from reading this piece of literature. For example, maybe the writing style is too wordy, or the ideas are too philosophical.
3. Review each list and select a focus for the info-commercial. Does it persuade people to read the piece of literature or does it persuade them not to read it?
4. Chart the plot. At the top of a large piece of construction paper, draw a line and label the parts of the classical dramatic structure on the appropriate spots.
5. Below each section, list the key points of action that are contained in each section. For example, all the background information needed for creating the context is listed under exposition; action that builds to the turning point is listed under rising action; under climax, the turning point is described; actions that follow the climax are listed under falling action; and the

final closing action that wraps everything up is listed under denouement.

Part 3

1. Select roles to perform in the info-commercial.
2. Write a script for the info-commercial.
3. Make a list of props to be used and decide how and from where to obtain these. Props might include special wardrobe.

Part 4

1. Rehearse the info-commercial.

Part 5

1. Perform the info-commercial.

Part 6

1. Audience members can use the Response Guide to record their immediate impressions as they are watching the info-commercials being performed.
2. Each group receives all the Response Guides after its performance is completed.

Part 7

1. After all the info-commercials have been performed, each group reviews the Response Guides to reflect on its creative work.
2. Each group collaboratively drafts a short essay that explains how the info-commercial might be changed to make it even more persuasive and to review connections to soil, soul, and society.

RESPONSE GUIDE

1. Literature title _____
2. The group wants people to read this literature.
   Yes   No
3. List reasons that you heard given for the above recommendation.
4. I will read this piece of literature because
   _____
5. I will not read this piece of literature because
   _____
6. What part of the classical dramatic structure was the most effective in this info-commercial?
   Exposition   Rising action   Climax   Falling action   Denouement
7. Soil, soul, and society were appropriately interconnected.
   No   Partially   Yes
8. Add other comments that may help the group strengthen its info-commercial.

CHAPTER 10

Cave Art: Is It Literature? Is It Writing?

Overview: This five-part activity involves film-viewing, drawing, discussing, researching, and writing about cave art. Participants decide if cave art is literature, writing, or both. History, environmental pressures on ancient human and animal populations, and the relationship of art to early-childhood (ages 2–7) language acquisition are embedded in the activities.[1]

Materials: Brown-paper lunch bags or grocery bags, markers or crayons, tape or DVD of the movie *Ice Age*, wall space, TV or VCR, paper and pen

Suggested Time: Part 1, 1 hour; Part 2, 1 hour; Part 3, 3–10 hours; Part 4, 5–10 hours

Participants: Individuals, partners, small groups

Types of Learning: Visual, verbal (written and spoken), physical, intellectual, emotional, spiritual, social, environmental, and reflective

Rhetorical Forms: Fiction, autobiography, report writing

Prerequisite: Access to a local library and/or Internet search engines; knowledge of source documentation style such as APA, MLA, or others

Precautions: The facilitator might want to present an overview of the entire activity for the purpose of selecting (with the participants) time guidelines on each part.

THE ACTIVITY

Part 1: For Individuals (1 hour)

1. Watch Scene 12 from the movie *Ice Age*.[2]
2. Discuss the movie clip. What was the cave art showing or saying?
3. Introduce and read a short story, for example, a fable or parable.
4. Pass out paper bags.
5. Instruct participants to crumple up their bags to give a cave look to their paper and then to smooth it back out flat.
6. Instruct participants now to draw their own cave art that depicts a fictional story or a story of their own lives.
7. As the art is completed, tape it to the wall space.
8. When all the cave art is on the wall, have each participant explain his or her story.

Part 2: Partner or Small-Group Collaboration (1 hour)

1. After the whole group discussion above, instruct participants to write a description of the cave art for an audience who has not yet seen it or who may never see it. The description should reveal physical, social, mental, aesthetic, emotional, and spiritual aspects that they see. The overall purpose of cave art and the activity to this point can also be included.

Part 3: Partner or Small-Group Collaboration in Research (time as needed in a library or on the Internet; 3–10 hours suggested)

1. Instruct participants to find facts about cave art in various parts of the world that they can use to compare and contrast with their own group cave art wall. These facts may also feature information about extinct species or human conditions.
2. Instruct participants to find facts about the role of art in early-childhood language acquisition and development.

3. Ask participants to take a position on whether cave art is literature or writing or perhaps both.

Part 4: Partner or Small-Group Synthesis and Collaboration in Report Writing (time is to be determined by the group; 5–10 hours suggested)

1. Instruct participants to collaborate as they write a report that interconnects their research with the cave art drawing and writing experience from Parts 1 and 2. Each partnership or small group produces one essay.

Part 5: Closure

1. Conduct a group discussion about the writing and discoveries that arose out of the writing.

REFERENCE

Donkin, J. C., Forte, L., & Meledander, C. (Producers) & Wedge, C., & Saldanha, C. (Directors). (2002). *Ice Age* [Motion Picture]. United States: 20th Century Fox.

NOTES

1. Samantha Clark and Tessa Holman (Central Michigan University students in English 460: Senior Seminar: Current Issues in English) designed Part 1 for use in first grade at the Austin Waldorf School. Parts 2, 3, and 4 make the activity suitable for an older and more experienced participant. Tessa and Sam's presentation of Part 1 during class presentations (Fall semester, 2004) went exceedingly well. After viewing the movie clip, an animated text, students stretched out on the floor or moved around to find a comfortable spot to draw their cave art. During the group discussion, we learned more about each other, since most of the art was autobiographical,

and ideas about extinct species and human cultural practices either lost or dropped expanded the discussion beyond English. The discussion became interdisciplinary in a natural way. I believe this activity facilitated interconnections and holistic learning very successfully without being forced or self-conscious. Tessa and Sam were delighted by my request to use their material and granted permission for me to do so.

2. This clip shows the characters observing cave art that depicts extinct species and family life among the species.

CHAPTER 11

Finding Your Community's Literature

Overview: This activity[1] broadens the understanding and place of writing in our everyday lives and in our community. Participants conduct a community field study to gather found literature. They then create a group collage and analyze the motivation, purpose, and expression of "found literature" in the community.

Materials: Cameras or digital cameras; computer, visualizer, or overhead projector; a big white sheet of paper and tape; pens, markers, paper, artifact documentation cards; stapler with staples, journals, magazines

Suggested Time: 60 minutes for preparation; community time to be determined by the group or facilitator; 60 minutes for sharing and discussion of found literature; 60 minutes for journal writing

Participants: Individuals, partners, small groups

Types of Learning: Visual, verbal (written and spoken), physical, intellectual, emotional, spiritual, social, environmental, and reflective

Rhetorical Forms: Journal writing

Prerequisite: Basic skills of reading and writing; operation of a camera or digital camera and the computer to upload pictures

Precautions: A handout identifying rules and restrictions for gathering found literature should be distributed prior to community exploration (see "Precautions and Reminders" at the end of this chapter).

THE ACTIVITY

Found literature can be seen by direct observation of written artifacts throughout the community. They are generally found embedded in other forms. For example, you might find a bulletin board with announcements of local events. A passage from one might strike you as particularly literary or poetic. Most often, found literature takes the shape of poetry. This makes "found poems" easier to see than other genres that require more length and detail.

When identifying a found poem, look for words that are sequenced so that meaning other than the surface or intended meaning might be seen. Usually, found literature is discovered within another piece of writing and is not the entire piece of writing it is found within. You cannot add words to the section you believe to be a "found piece of literature." So this means a found piece of literature is a segment of a larger piece and is intact within the larger piece. It can be a string of words, phrases, or sentences.

Found literature can also be discovered by omitting words, phrases, or sentences within the sequence. For example, sentence 3 of the original might be sentence 1 of your found piece, and the original sentence 6 might be sentence 2 of the found piece.

Discovering found literature requires seeing written artifacts in new order and with new meaning. It means looking at billboards, signs, advertisements, fliers, posters, newspaper articles, nonfiction pieces, technical reports, graffiti, and all genres of written expression with a new set of eyes.

Part 1: Preparation for Community Field Work

The facilitator should:

1. Introduce and describe the purpose and directions of the activity.
2. Distribute handouts and allow questions.
3. Encourage students to work with others.

4. Distribute a magazine to each person and instruct him or her to look for found literature. This is a warm-up for when they are engaged in community fieldwork.
5. Review genres of written expression participants might consider when in the field.
6. Allow time for students to make a plan of action for field work. For example, they might make a list of possible places to visit and types of genres to look for or at. They might make a timetable that shows when, where, and with whom they visit that site. They might make a list of materials they need to take along on their field study.
7. Review and give instructions about gathering material in the field.

Part 2: Community Fieldwork

1. Allow the participants time for locating found literature in the community.
2. Instruct them to take photographs of the original written artifacts.

If photographs are too difficult or impossible to get, instruct participants to record their originals in a notebook for later reference. While photographs are *exact* reference points from which the setting or context of the found literature is understood, a written record of the same suffices. This information is needed when forming a synthesis about the community as discussed in Part 4.

Part 3: Forming a Collage

1. Have participants share their collected found literature. They should identify the genre and tell where it was found. They can also speculate on what motivated the literature and what emotions and meaning are evoked in the newfound literature once it is seen.
2. Create a collage or bulletin board of all the collected artifacts.

Part 4: Community Synthesis

1. Have participants write a short analysis of the collage.
2. The facilitator might want the group to generate a list of issues they can consider before synthesizing the collage.
3. What does the collage say about literature? What does it say about the place of writing in our community? What does it say about the community? What does it say about the places it was found? What does it say about the people who found it? What general impression about the community can a non–community member receive from the collage?
4. What message might someone receive about soul, soil, and society after reflecting on separate parts of the collage and/or on the whole collage?

PRECAUTIONS AND REMINDERS

While you are exploring your community for found literature, keep these things in mind:

Do

1. Tell your guardian where you are going and for what reason.
2. Always get permission before leaving.
3. Do your searching during daylight hours only.
4. Go in a group of people. Have friends or family members join you on your journey.

Do Not

1. Trespass onto private property.
2. Take pieces that are in use or have been placed for a purpose (e.g., if you see a flyer posted on a bulletin board do not rip it down; instead, take a picture of it).

3. Cause disturbances (e.g., do not speak loudly when searching through a library).

Good Places

Churches
Community centers
Libraries and schools
Sidewalks
Bulletin boards

Bad Places

Bars
Warehouses
Construction sites
Alleyways
Dumpsters

Smart People Make Smart Decisions

NOTE

1. This activity, originally titled "Your Community's Literature," was created by Joel D. Annunzio, Kelly Stevens, Emily Homrich, and Susanne Peck from English 460: Senior Seminar: Issues in English. I have used it with their permission, but I have extensively modified it. The collage they created during their class presentation stimulated a lot of interesting discussion about community values and environmental conditions that shape people and communities.

CHAPTER 12

Creating a Life's Legacy

Overview: This activity[1] requires participants to set future goals by which their life is judged at the time of their death. They are encouraged to produce a personal connection between time, death, and epitaphs as a form of legacy. They read, interpret, and discuss famous epitaphs as a prelude to writing their own. They plan future goals that can lead to a significant legacy that is summarized or symbolized in some way by their epitaph. They then write their own epitaphs and volunteer it to be read aloud to them by others. A more extensive writing follows.

Materials: Pen and paper; a mat or blanket; samples of poems and famous epitaphs (see "Anonymous Epitaphs" and "Epitaphs of Famous Authors" at the end of this chapter); construction paper for making epitaphs; markers or crayons

Suggested Time: 1–2 hours for Parts 1, 2, and 3, followed by sufficient writing time

Participants: Individuals, small groups

Types of Learning: Visual, verbal (written and spoken), physical, intellectual, emotional, spiritual, social, environmental, and reflective

Rhetorical Forms: This activity could lead to a number of written genres, for example, songs, poems, short stories, plays that enact the goals, reflective or analytic essays, process essays of instructions to reach the goals, letters to parents, siblings, or children, and journal writing.

Prerequisite: Familiarity with the scene from Mark Twain's (1999) *The Adventures of Tom Sawyer* when Tom witnesses his own funeral. Familiarity with the way time influences setting and cultural attitudes.

Precautions: It is imperative to stay focused on life and the quality of life, rather than on death. A person's ability to recognize his or her soul, follow its demands, contribute to society, and sustain our Earth should be featured in discussions. The epitaph, emphasized as a legacy, makes a statement about life, not death, and it can awaken a new awareness of what can be manifested in life.

THE ACTIVITY

Part 1: Literary Preparation (Small Groups or One Large Group)

1. Review Tom Sawyer's funeral scene from *The Adventures of Tom Sawyer* (Chapter 17). Discussion needs to include issues of time and its relevance to the people and their attitudes about Tom's life. Tom's ability to self-reflect and to develop new awareness about his life can assist in creating the strong emphasis on life that is needed in this activity.
2. Define *epitaph*, its ability to leave a legacy, and its cultural importance.
3. Review epitaphs of famous authors, speculate about the person's life, and identify the legacy left by the epitaph (see at the end of this chapter).

Part 2: Planning the Legacy (Individuals)

1. Make a plan for your life's legacy. Identify achievements, goals, and personal and professional characteristics to develop. Create a timeline for manifesting this plan.
2. Write an epitaph that symbolizes or summarizes your life's legacy.
3. Cut out a headstone shape from the construction paper and write the epitaph on it. Illustrate it accordingly, if desired.

Part 3: Sharing the Legacy (Whole Group and Individuals)

1. Read aloud the epitaphs.

Part 4: Writing About the Legacy (Individuals)

1. Allow time for journal writing.
2. Allow time for an extended writing in a particular genre. All writing should include additional development of the participant's plan to manifest his or her personal legacy.

ANONYMOUS EPITAPHS (HOME.WI.RR.COM/EPITAPHS)

She skied—But loved the sea
yet loved her family more
Thus she quietly waits
in this beautiful place
for those who love
the mountains and the snow
Oct. 21, 1916–July 23, 1976

Playing with names in a Ruidos, New Mexico, cemetery:
Here lies Johnny Yeast. Pardon me for not rising.

A lawyer's epitaph in England:
Sir John Strange
Here lies an honest lawyer, And that is Strange.

On Margaret Daniel's grave at Hollywood Cemetery, Richmond, Virginia:
She always said her feet were killing her but nobody believed her.

Anna Hopewell's grave in Enosburg Falls, Vermont, has an epitaph that sounds like something from a *Three Stooges* movie:

Here lies the body of our Anna
Done to death by a banana
It wasn't the fruit that laid her low
But the skin of the thing that made her go.

From the gravestone of John White, London:
Here lies John
A burning shining light
Whose name, life and actions
Were all alike
All white

Love only knoweth
whence it came and
comprehendith love
March 6, 1854–March 7, 1878

One by one earth's ties are broken as we see our love decay and the hopes so fondly cherished Brighten but to pass away one by one our hopes grow brighter as we near the shining shore for we know across the river wait the loved ones gone before.

April 21, 1890, 53 years, 3 months, 17 days
So few realize what life is about.
If I knew nothing else, I knew warmth, pleasure,
Despite everything, I knew love.
People look for what they can measure:
A degree, money, children they can brag about,
Reasons others might wish them mazel tov.
On days like other days were moments I treasured,
Life like other lives, humdrum, passing without
Yammering, with you, with the children, full enough. . .

EPITAPHS OF FAMOUS AUTHORS
(WWW.FAMOUSQUOTES.ME.UK/EPITAPHS)

Good Friend for Jesus Sake Forbeare To
Digg the Dust Encloased Heare
Blest Be Ye Man Yt Spares Thes Stones and
Curst Be He Yt Moves My Bones
   William Shakespeare

Workers of All Lands Unite.
The Philosophers Have Only Interpreted the World in Various Ways; The Point is to Change it.
   Karl Marx

The body of Benjamin Franklin, printer (like the cover of an old book, its contents worn out, and stripped of its lettering and gilding) lies here, food for worms. Yet the work itself shall not lost, for it will, as he believed, appear once more In a new and more beautiful edition, corrected and amended by its Author
   Benjamin Franklin

Against You I Will Fling Myself,
Unvanquished And Unyielding, O Death!
   Virginia Woolf

Called Back.
   Emily Dickinson

Quoth the Raven,
Nevermore.
   Edgar Allen Poe

I had a Lover's Quarrel with The World.
   Robert Frost

Nothing in Moderation,
We All Loved Him.
  Ernie Kovacs

If [the writer] achieves anything noble, anything enduring,
it must be by giving himself absolutely to his material. . . .
He fades away into the land and people of his heart,
He dies of love only to be born again.
  Willa Cather

REFERENCE

Twain, M. (1999). *The adventures of Tom Sawyer*. New York: Children's Classics.

NOTE

1. This activity has been adapted from work completed by Elizabeth Shamus, Nikki Frazier, and Janae Goodchild, students in English 460: Senior Seminar: Current Issues in English, Fall 2004. They believed it would fit the curriculum in place at the Community School in Camden, Maine.

CHAPTER 13

Music and Dance to Inspire the Pen

Overview: This activity contains five parts that culminate in a written experience that is based on music, dance, discussion, performance, and sharing. It contains multicultural aspects that can include Internet or library research. It asks participants to fine-tune their perceptions and to understand the power of implication and inference. Participant choice is strongly featured, but the activity begins with a facilitator setting a particular tone and process for analyzing and responding to music and dance as cultural information. Depending on the music and dance selections, this activity can feature soil, soul, and society quite easily.

Materials: Music and dance selections and the equipment to hear and see it, paper and pen, space for movement

Suggested Time: Part 1, 2–4 hours; Part 2, 1–3 hours; Part, 4–10 hours, depending on time selected for music, research, and writing; Part 4, 10–15 minutes for each performance, total time depends on whole group size; Part 5, 2–6 hours or as determined by participants

Participants: Individuals and partners

Types of Learning: Visual, verbal (written and spoken), auditory, physical, intellectual, emotional, spiritual, social, environmental, and reflective

Rhetorical Forms: Essay, other self-selected genres possible

Prerequisite: None

Precautions: Participants choosing to create their own music and dance should be encouraged to avoid cultural forms that are based on lewd suggestions, misogyny, violence, or nudity.

THE ACTIVITY

Part 1: Facilitator Preparation

The facilitator needs to:

1. Select two to three examples of music or videos of dance from foreign places. These should be short enough to experience in one or two sessions.
2. Write a list of factual characteristics of the people (to be used as a handout further on).
3. List the instruments used in the music (to be used as a handout further on).
4. Identify the type of dance in the video and its cultural purpose (to be used as a handout further on).

Part 2: Participant Warm-Up Writing

1. Participants listen to the music and/or see the dance video, and in small groups or with a partner create a speculative profile of the people in that place which is implied by the music or dance. A list of characteristics is sufficient at this point.
2. The facilitator then passes out a list of characteristics previously compiled that is based on geographical and cultural fact. A list of instruments used in the music and/or types of dance and their purpose is also needed, since some of the sounds may be unfamiliar to the participants.
3. Participants review the "facts" and compare it with their "speculations." They need to identify specific elements in the music or dance that led to their speculations.

These elements might include but are not limited to the following:

Rhythm
Sound
Types of instruments
Numbers of instruments
Beat
Volume
Pitch
Male voices
Female voices
Sounds from nature such as bird calls, wind, rain, or waves
Body postures
Dance steps
Dance costumes
Cadence
Minor or major key
Duration of music and/or dance
Blend of music and dance
Visual sets
Space restrictions
Number of dancers
Solos, duets, and so on
Orchestration

This writing may take the form of a list, paragraph, or short essay.

4. After the discussion, participants may write a short response that identifies what they learned about:

Drawing inferences
Reaching conclusions
Perception shifts
The importance of voice, movement, and visuals
The atmosphere without facts

The atmosphere with facts
Making meaning with movement and sound
The advantage of standing outside a culture
The advantage of standing inside a culture

Part 3: The Personal Self and Cultural Identity

1. Each individual now selects a piece of music or dance *or* creates new, original music or dance that reveals something about his or her own personality and culture.
2. The individual completes two short writings:

    A list of facts about the music or dance (as written above in #4). Participants can use the Internet or library to gather additional factual information at this point.
    A short explanation of how specific elements imply or infer identity, culture, or atmosphere.

3. Participants find a partner for the next few steps and complete the following:

    They exchange music or dance videos in order to repeat the steps in Part 2.
    They discuss their speculations afterward.

Part 4: Sharing Profiles and Culture

1. Each partnership will "show and tell" their music or dance video to the larger group and speak to specific issues they select to showcase from this activity.

or

2. Each partnership performs their original music and dance and then speak to specific issues that they wish to showcase from their experience.

Part 5: Writing With the Inspired Pen

1. Participants can write alone or with a partner. They select the organizational strategies that they wish to use in the essay.
2. After Part 4 has ended, participants may write an essay that identifies what they learned about:

   Drawing inferences
   Reaching conclusions
   Perception shifts
   The importance of voice, movement, and visuals
   The atmosphere without facts
   The atmosphere with facts
   Making meaning with movement and sound
   The advantage of standing outside a culture
   The advantage of standing inside a culture
   The pressure and challenge of performance
   The joy of performing
   Similarities between writing, dance, and music

or

3. They may select an alternate rhetorical genre that suits their goal as they express their whole experience with writing, dance, and music.

CHAPTER 14

The Writer's Scrapbook

Overview: In this activity,[1] participants read a collection of non-fiction essays and create a scrapbook of collages that presents specific ideas and images from each essay. Each collage represents a different essay and depicts what the reader envisioned in their "mind's eye" when they read the essay. Images include headlines and/or captions that enlighten a reader of the scrapbook about the relationship between the images, the written prose, and the scrapbook author's vision. This activity leads participants to a better understanding of the emotional power images evoke, particularly the images embedded in written prose. A written commentary explaining each page of the scrapbook documents the scrapbook. The completed scrapbook becomes a memory book containing emotionally moving or theme-centered mini-collages.

Materials: One scrapbook; various magazines from which images can be cut; a collection of creative nonfiction prose essays (e.g., *The Art of the Personal Essay* [Kitchen, 2005] or *Short Takes: Brief Encounters With Contemporary Nonfiction* [Lopate, 1995]); paper and pen; scrapbook supplies such as scissors, glue, paste, tape, glitter, construction paper, markers, plastic page protectors, and so on; computer software such as Broderbund's The Print Shop

Suggested Time: 40–50 hours

Participants: Individuals or partners

Types of Learning: Visual, verbal (written and spoken), physical, intellectual, emotional, spiritual, social, environmental, and reflective

Rhetorical Forms: Narration that includes process, information, evaluation, and analysis

Prerequisite: None

Precautions: This activity may require participants to read the essays more than once. Time management should accommodate this possibility.

THE ACTIVITY

Part 1: Selecting Specific Passages

Highlight passages that are emotionally moving, interesting, or relevant for depicting soul, soil, and society themes. You will want to use three or four passages in each collage. You may want to select twice as many passages as you need just in case you cannot find images for a particular passage.

Part 2: Finding Images and Creating Captions

This step requires careful time management:

1. Search for pictures and images that integrate the "feeling" of the quote into colors and images.
2. Consider using a software program that lets you create greeting cards, stationary, posters, and so on, such as Broderbund's The Print Shop v. 20.0, which has over 750,000 images, photos, and templates, all in accordance to the Licensing Agreement. Be prepared to spend time searching and sorting before selecting. This can become an endless time commitment. Try to set a shorter time limit, 3 hours perhaps, and see what you get.

3. Be prepared to use an alternative quote if you cannot find an appropriate image to match quotes you first selected.
4. Consider using old magazines or mail-order catalogs.
5. Consider using newspaper headlines when creating captions. Captions should be relevant and show the connections between your vision and the literature and/or the theme of soul, soil, and society.
6. Consider using old photographs of your own that can be permanently attached in the scrapbook.
7. Consider drawing your own image.
8. Consider creating images out of fabric, natural materials such as leaves, twigs, and items from nature.
9. There are a lot of ways for creating images. Free your imagination and do something new.

Part 3: Creating the Collage and Compiling the Scrapbook

This step can also be very time consuming. Plan for 6–8 hours minimum.

1. You need heavy stock construction paper to hold the images that form each collage.
2. Mat each picture in a unique way that is artistic and beautiful.
3. Supplement each collage with the adjoining quote and/or caption.
4. You could use clear plastic page protectors for the finished collage.
5. Arrange each collage in an order that makes sense to you.
6. Give your scrapbook an original title.

Part 4: The Written Commentary

The written commentary should include the following parts:

1. A description of the process used when creating the scrapbook
2. Reasons for literary selections

3. Reasons for image selections
4. Reasons for headline or caption selections
5. An analysis of the relationship between images and words
6. A statement that declares what was learned and the degree of satisfaction gained by completing the activity
7. Suggestions for improving the activity

Part 5: Show and Tell

This part is optional, but it is without question a useful part of the activity to include if time allows. People who spend a good amount of time building their scrapbook will want to show it off and talk about how it influenced their understanding of the literature.

REFERENCES

Kitchen, J. (Ed.). (2005). *Short takes: Brief encounters with contemporary nonfiction.* New York: Norton.

Lopate, P. (Ed.). (1995). *The art of the personal essay.* New York: Anchor.

NOTE

1. I am grateful to Carrie Lake, who created a fine scrapbook that featured four short stories and five novels by the American writer Willa Cather. Carrie's scrapbook provides superb support for using a holistic approach. When assigned a creative project as a final class project in English 345: Studies in Authors, Carrie turned to what she loves to do, scrapbooking, as a means of synthesizing her experiences with the literature. She demonstrated ways students move far beyond the scope of an assignment when they are free to make choices and design the direction of their own learning experience. Carrie's response to the assignment is partially used here with her permission.

CHAPTER 15
Voice and Identity: The Sound of Respect

Overview: Participants write a creative nonfiction essay about the quality and/or development of voice and identity as it is embedded in an expression of respect. Respect can happen in small personal ways or in large universal ways. When we think of respect, we probably first think of respect that is shown by one person for another, but respect can also be demonstrated between large groups of people, nations, ecosystems, financial systems, political systems, religions, biological systems, and so on. The participant needs to select the context, experience, or event within which respect is the primary feature. Soil, soul, and society can easily be interconnected or embedded. Some research to gather truthful facts might be necessary depending on choices made, but personal knowledge alone can also be appropriate.

Materials: The Fourth Genre by Robert L. Root Jr. and Michael Steinberg (2005), paper and pen, television, radio, small notebook for keeping notes

Suggested Time: To be arranged by the facilitator and participant

Participants: Individuals

Types of Learning: Verbal (written and spoken), intellectual, emotional, spiritual, social, environmental, and reflective

Rhetorical Forms: Creative nonfiction essay. Possible forms of creative nonfiction to choose from are memoir, nature essay, personal essay, segmented essay, critical essay, and literary journalism.

Prerequisite: An introduction to the fourth literary genre, creative nonfiction. Participants need to be familiar with the various forms of creative nonfiction before starting this activity. To simplify the activity, the facilitator could choose one form and have all participants focus on that one. A more democratic approach would be to introduce all the forms to the participants, let them choose which one to use, *or* to vote on whether everyone should use the same form.

Precautions: None

THE ACTIVITY

Part 1: Points to Remember About Creative Nonfiction[1]

1. The personal presence of the writer is seen or felt in creative nonfiction.
2. Self-discovery and self-exploration are encouraged in creative nonfiction. The form is very flexible and pushes against the boundaries of fiction and poetry. Possible forms of creative nonfiction to choose from are memoir, nature essay, personal essay, segmented essay, critical essay, and literary journalism.
3. Content should be truthful, rather than fictional, to a degree that satisfies the rhetorical purpose of the writing.
4. Autobiography, history, journalism, biology, ecology, travel writing, medicine, and others may offer a framework or subject matter within which the self-exploration or self-discovery is contained.
5. Any literary element that is usually seen in fiction, poetry, and drama can be used when writing a creative nonfiction essay.
6. Creative nonfiction often utilizes the lyrical, dramatic, meditative, expository, and argumentative elements.
7. Innovative or experimental structure is often seen in creative nonfiction. This can include surprising ways of organizing narrative and chronology.
8. Language is literary and imaginative.

9. When writing creative nonfiction, it is helpful to think of the essay as a journey—for the writer and the reader—that leads to a significant point of surprise or discovery.

Part 2: Possible Connections With Soil, Soul, and Society

When selecting a context, experience, or event, mine the soil, soul, and society trinity as a source of inspiration and interconnection. A little brainstorming can offer a start. A few ideas that could feature soil:

1. Animal testing
2. Water conservancy
3. Land management
4. Gardening
5. Crop rotation
6. Herbicide and pesticide use
7. Water treatment plants
8. Growing and preserving food

A few ideas that feature soul:

1. Joy and personal satisfaction from growing flowers or vegetables
2. Respect for a special piece of music that has inspired or soothed
3. Donating blood
4. A transcendental moment in nature
5. A challenge nature has imposed that has been overcome
6. An act of kindness and/or generosity that overwhelms
7. A piece of art that awakens our imaginations
8. A sublime moment of faith in another person

A few ideas drawn from society:

1. Ways United Nations members show respect
2. Collaboration among businesses that depend on each other for survival, for example, relationship between trucking and grocery supply

3. The role of respect in a peace negotiation between warring nations
4. The role of respect in union negotiations
5. Respect in our judicial system
6. Respect in our medical system
7. Respect in city council meetings, or other governmental decision-making bodies
8. Religious tolerance in the United States

Part 3: Finding a Topic and Prewriting Preparation

1. Brainstorm and select a topic.
2. In a sentence or two, identify the level of respect demonstrated by this topic.
3. In a few sentences or questions, attempt to identify the type of voice you want to use or the one you think might be used. Name it and describe its qualities. What do you want to learn about your voice as it functions in relation to this topic?
4. In a few sentences or questions, address identity in the same way you did voice. What do you expect to discover? What would you like to discover?
5. Write a brief passage that describes the interconnections to soil, soul, and society.
6. List all the facts you have about your subject. If you do not have enough, take time to learn more about your topic. Expand your list of facts.

Part 4: Selecting a Form

1. Choose from memoir, nature essay, personal essay, segmented essay, critical essay, and literary journalism.
2. Creative nonfiction often utilizes the lyrical, dramatic, meditative, expository, and argumentative elements.
3. It may be helpful at this point to look at published models of that form, especially if you are trying something for the first time. Refer to *The Fourth Genre* (Root & Steinberg, 2005) for models.

Part 5: Writing the First Draft

1. Refer to your prewriting preparation as you start.
2. Let your intuition blend with your facts as you shape your essay.
3. Be open to surprises and unexpected discovery.
4. Do not worry so much about form correctness at this stage. Be willing to shift into an alternate form if the essay goes in that direction.
5. Do not aim for any particular length. Let the writing guide that.
6. End the first draft after you have reached a point of satisfaction and discovery is *evident*.

Part 6: Revising the Draft

Check the essay for the following:

1. A point of discovery or surprise is included.
2. The writer's personal presence is felt or heard.
3. Voice and identity are evident, either explicitly or implicitly. An explicit occurrence occurs when voice and/or identity are part of the topic and are discussed within the essay. An implicit occurrence occurs when voice and/or identity are heard and felt when a reader reads the essay.
4. Connections to soil, soul, and society are included.
5. The form meets the rhetorical conventions inherent in that form, but may also be experimental or imaginative.
6. The language is literary and imaginative.
7. The facts are truthful.
8. Literary elements, such as metaphor or figurative language, are used.
9. The essay has something significant to say about the topic.
10. The essay provides readers with a sense of self-discovery or self-exploration.
11. Rewrite where and as often as is necessary or desirable.

REFERENCE

Root, R. L., Jr., & Steinberg, M. (Eds.). (2005). *The fourth genre: Contemporary writers of/on creative nonfiction* (3rd ed.). New York: Pearson Longman.

NOTE

1. See the introduction to *The Fourth Genre* for a more detailed discussion of each of these points.

CHAPTER 16

Writing the Outdoors: 3 Days in Nature

Overview: An extended 3-day (or longer) gathering can occur during a camping trip or at a lodge resort if camping is undesirable to the participants. It is essential to select a site that is accessible to nature. This site can be local or at a distance. The learning purposes of each group help determine site location. Why a minimum of 3 days? An extended time together offers multiple opportunities for holistic educational experiences and can be shaped to meet the special interests of the participants. The trinity of soil, soul, and society automatically and naturally arises. Preparation, planning, and cost can be shared by all the participants. The main intention of this 3-day outdoor learning activity is to introduce the participants to basic attitudes and beliefs about the environment and their connection to it that they may not have yet considered.

Materials: Determined by site qualities and activities selected during pre-event preparation

Suggested Time: Friday through Sunday; *or* three consecutive weekdays

Participants: Groups

Types of Learning: Verbal (written and spoken), auditory, visual, intellectual, emotional, spiritual, social, environmental, and reflective

Rhetorical Forms: Journal writing and other types as determined by the participants

Prerequisite: Extensive preparation; possibly fundraising. It is imperative that the group facilitator have environmental or ecological knowledge and be able to share that knowledge with group participants, because learners are likely to remember knowledge and learn faster from a mentor. The group facilitator may retain the role of knowledge seeker and learner, but should in some way be more knowledgeable than the group participants, especially if a long-term change in attitude and behavior is a purpose.

Precautions: Poll participants for information such as allergies, personal preferences, and so on. Other precautions are determined by site qualities and previous outdoor experience of the participants. For instance, during white-water rafting everyone should have a life preserver and helmet, or when camping during summer, those allergic to bee stings should carry medication and inform the group facilitator of their allergy ahead of time in case a bee sting occurs. A list of precautions can be generated *before* the event takes place. A 3-day outdoor learning experience is not for everyone and no person should be forced to go along. An alternative to the activity should be offered by the facilitator or created and suggested by the participant.

THE ACTIVITY

Foreword: Why Outdoor Learning

The extensive literature on outdoor learning is generally divided into adventure education and environmental education. Adventure education places students into some level of real or perceived risk so that when they successfully meet challenges they experience growth. Environmental education provides knowledge about and experiences in nature as a means to change people into ecological stewards and activists.

Research by Glenda Hanna (1995) and others indicate that "recreational experiences play an important role in influencing higher levels of environmental concern and activism" (p. 22). Today it is generally accepted that providing children and young adults with direct experiences in nature lead to a stronger appreciation and understanding of ecology. Moreover, a study reported by Hanna (1995) indicates "that it is important to develop a positive, ecocentric wilderness attitude through cognitive channels as well as through affective and physical channels" (p. 29). In other words, a holistic approach to learning the outdoors by being in the outdoors has a greater impact on learners than does classroom experience alone.

When learners have direct contact with the outdoors, something magical happens for many of them. They develop a new sense of awe and wonder about the planet Earth and about their relationship with it. They begin to recognize the power of place and the way place shapes personal and cultural identity. They have the opportunity to change attitudes and behaviors about the Earth and about how her resources are used. Learners awaken in dramatic, at times sublime, ways that reconnect them to beauty and to life. They may awaken to self and spirit.

Not all learners have a dramatic or spiritual awakening in nature. Participants who have internalized a competitive consumerist approach to life may have difficulty observing the subtle beauty that is in nature. The "drama" in nature may not be as loud or as fast as an action film at their local theater. Some people prefer shopping trips and fast-food eateries and have difficulty adjusting to a new set of challenges, particularly those designed by nature.

Pre-trip preparation can establish realistic expectations for those who are not so inclined to feel comfortable in nature. It is part of the facilitator's role to discuss the ups and downs of outdoor learning and to begin building a sense of community so that, if it becomes necessary, an uncomfortable participant knows whom to turn to for support. The facilitator needs to bring the participants to accept the idea that education is not simply something than happens indoors.

According to Laura Parker Roerden (2001), "fewer than 10 percent of our children in the United States today learn about nature by being in nature. More than half learn about the natural world through technology and the rest from inside a classroom" (p. 60). Her attempts to teach science through an extensive scuba diving field trip has met with success and significantly changed students as it has changed her. She testifies that (Roerden, 2001)

> when you teach outside, what I think of as a "third presence" emerges, guiding and informing the learning—the earth itself will seemingly have a voice. When I've surrendered to this feeling, I've noticed my own passions reawakened. I've found the job of being all-knowing teacher impossible—nature reveals herself as too complex. Mysteries I do not yet understand reengage me as a learner. My sense of wonder and curiosity is renewed. Nature is not only the classroom, it is the teacher. The earth protects us, nurtures us, tells us about the shape of our heart, and we in kind are called to do the same for the earth. (p. 63)

As David Orr (1992) tells us, the goal of ecological literacy "is not just a comprehension of how the world works, but in the light of that knowledge, a life lived accordingly" (p. 87). Orr (1992) further tells us that there are some common elements shared among those who are more comfortable with the environment: "experience in the natural world at an early age" (p. 88); the presence of an "older teacher or mentor as a role model; and seminal books that explain, heighten, and say what we have felt deeply" (p. 88). The facilitation of an outdoor learning activity can be grounded by establishing experience with these common elements.

Part 1: Intention and Purpose

Early preparation for any outdoor learning experience requires specific decisions and time allowances that prepare the facilitator(s) and the participants.

1. A clear intention for the trip should be articulated. Will it be an "adventure" or "environmental" educational experience? Or,

can the trip be designed in a way to accommodate both adventure and environmental education?
2. In what way are the participants challenged?
3. What are participants expected to learn?
4. How might they change, and is change short-term or long-term?
5. How might change be recognized or measured?

Part 2: Date and Site Selection

The time of year for the 3-day adventure and specific site qualities will determine the sorts of equipment needed as well as the direction the learning experiences might take or its focus.

The participants need to select a weekend date before selecting a site. When reserving space, the exact dates are needed. If the group is free to go during the week, campground and/or resort rates are often lower. Pros and cons:

> Springtime is milder, with fewer bugs. Usually spring is considered preseason and rates are often lower. Sites are generally in less demand and therefore less crowded. The weather can be unpredictable, rainy, cold, or cloudy. Water temperature in lakes and rivers is lower, even icy in certain parts of the country or at high altitudes. Hiking and biking trails can be muddy or impassable. Nights are cooler. Pollens can be uncomfortable for those with asthma or hay fever.
> Summer months provide the most predictable and temperate weather. Bugs can be a nuisance. Rates are at the highest. Water temperature is usually warm enough for swimming or other water activities. Trails are generally well groomed and accessible. Nights are warmer. Pollens can be higher and uncomfortable for those with asthma or hay fever.
> Fall months are generally drier than spring and offer warm days and cool, even crisp, nights. Rates may be lower than during

summer months but still a bit higher than during spring. Trails are still accessible. Bugs such as mosquitoes or flies are less problematic. Pollens have generally calmed down, but leaf mold can be a problem for those with allergies.

Winter months are colder. Travel can be hazardous and unpredictable. Campers can be at risk even with the right equipment if a storm comes on. Rates are low and sites are generally empty or underutilized. Bugs are gone. There are fewer daylight hours. The challenge to survive offers a higher level of success and satisfaction. Trails are often inaccessible except by snowshoes or skis. Lakes and rivers can be frozen.

The participants need to select a wilderness location. Longer travel time means less site time and higher expense. A location not more than four hours (by car) from home is reasonable.

The participants need to decide if they want to camp and if so what sort of camping. For example, will they backpack to a more remote spot or will they car camp (vehicles are parked next to campsite)? Will they tent camp or camp in recreational vehicles? Will they camp in a county park or a state park? Will the campground offer flush toilets and showers or pit toilets? Will the campground offer electricity for recreational vehicles? Most states have an 800 number for state campground reservations. Most county parks do not require or accept reservations and offer space on a first-come-first-served basis. Pros and cons:

Tent camping or backpacking requires sleeping on the ground, setting up a tent, and cooking over an open fire or camp stove. The biggest advantage (or disadvantage, depending on point of view) to this type of adventure is that participants are out of doors *all of the time*. Even when sleeping in a tent, there is a sense of being outdoors because there are not four walls and a roof or floor. Naturally, weather conditions can cause interesting challenges, to say the least. The ability to stay warm and dry is important, as is the availability of drinking water and personal hygiene options. After being out of doors for an extended time period, some participants may have difficulty reassimilating to indoor living after the trip.

The participants need to decide if they prefer an adventure weekend at a resort lodge, rather than a campout experience. All across the country there are resorts and lodges for daily, weekend, weekly, and even monthly rental. Most come fully equipped with bedding, kitchens, bathrooms, fireplaces, firewood, and so on. The extent of amenities is usually included in the property descriptions, and if something is lacking, it often can be negotiated. Some places give discount prices during off-seasons and/or for educational groups.

Protection from bad weather is the strongest advantage, but others include beds, showers and flush toilets, kitchen facilities, heating system, running water, and various amenities one associates with a hotel or home. If weather is bad, it also might mean that everyone is reluctant to go out of doors, and if there are too many people for the space, nerves can get stretched. Noise levels may also get too high, and privacy may be harder to find. Participants need to be more assertive about being in nature and mini-lessons that require outdoor learning need to be facilitated. A resort or lodge is usually more expensive.

Part 3: Types of Possible Trips

As part of the planning process, participants can brainstorm about the type of trip that appeals to them and which is also feasible. The type of trip that is finally selected should interconnect with dates and site selection. A few suggestions are listed below:

1. River rafting
2. Tent camping
3. Silent retreat in the country

4. Mountain hiking
5. Canoeing a local river
6. Apple picking
7. Visiting a virgin forest
8. Visiting the birthplace of a famous author, musician, or painter
9. Historic forts
10. Bird sanctuaries
11. Wildlife preserve
12. Ski trips
13. Harvest time at an organic farm
14. Planting time at an organic farm
15. Searching the sky for star constellations
16. Native American powwows or festivals
17. A writer's weekend: time to write
18. A reader's weekend: share your favorite book and author
19. An adventure of identity and sharing: a 3-day focus on knowing the terrain and each other
20. Service work in a near-distant community

Find and select a focus, a purpose, one that suits the particular group of participants.

Part 4: Funding the Trip

A number of funding options exist.

1. Participants equally share the total cost.
2. Donations are requested from local organizations such as The Moose, The Elk, The Rotary Club, etc.
3. Sponsors are secured from among local businesses.
4. Donations for funds are made from local churches.
5. Schools sometimes have "field trip" funds set aside.
6. Funding is requested from parents and/or other relatives.
7. Specific fundraising projects, such as car washing, yard work, bake sales, or bottle drive are conducted by the participants.

Anyone wishing to participate should not be turned away due to cost.

Part 5: Identify Special Needs

There are usually special needs attached to any group. These should be identified and a plan put into place to accommodate them *before* arriving at the destination.

Part 6: Gathering the Food

The amount and types of food are determined by the number in the group as well as by the type of adventure the group has selected. If refrigeration is lacking, coolers and ice may be necessary, but when backpacking, coolers and ice are not an option. Some resorts or lodges also provide meals. First, it is necessary to select a site and type of adventure before identifying and securing food needs. Once the group has reached that point, the following process can help:

1. List all meals

    Friday, dinner
    Friday, snack
    Saturday, breakfast
    Saturday, lunch
    Saturday, dinner
    Saturday, snack
    Sunday, breakfast
    Sunday, lunch
    Sunday, return road trip snacks

2. List special needs

    Number of vegetarians
    Types of food allergies

Alternatives to foods like milk or cheese for those who need them

Meat alternatives for vegetarians

3. Prepare menus for each meal
4. Determine quantity needed
5. Equally share the responsibility of providing the food
6. Estimate cost of food and add this to the total trip cost

Part 7: Equipment Lists

The equipment that is brought along is partially determined by the type of trip that is chosen. The process below can help:

1. Make a complete list of equipment that is needed.
2. Create two categories: individual and group need.
3. Let each individual meet his or her own need for individual items such as toothbrush, sleeping bag, etc.
4. Share the responsibility for providing the other pieces of equipment that become communal equipment, such as camp stove, three coolers, three frying pans, matches, etc. Identify who brings each item.

Part 8: Extended Invitations

Certain age groups need additional attention, especially when it is a mixed-gender group. Extending invitations to others can help meet these needs. Consider inviting:

1. Parents
2. Grandparents
3. Neighbors
4. Older siblings
5. Other adult facilitators

Once extended invitations have been accepted, a group meeting to name and agree to certain behavioral policies is helpful. It sets boundaries and lets people know ahead of time what can happen if these boundaries are trespassed.

Part 9: Liability Issues

Liability issues exist for all age groups, but particular issues exist for underage participants. The facilitator needs to consider the following:

1. Parental or guardian permission forms
2. Transportation insurance
3. Accident insurance
4. Procedures to use if needed. (For example, if the lead facilitator is called away to the hospital with an injured participant, the facilitator's replacement selected ahead of time can cut down on stress during a crisis. The group can identify such procedures during the general meeting about expected behavioral policies.)

Part 10: Suggestions for Writing Activities

The writing activities can also be determined by the participants; perhaps one group wants to write intensively, while another group wants to keep writing to a minimum. At the very least, participants should bring journals for an amount of daily writing they self-select. Other activities might include the following:

1. Letters to relatives or friends
2. Nature writing
3. Evaluation recommendations at the end of the adventure trip
4. Responses to reading selections
5. Responses to others' writing

6. Collaborative writing
7. Creative writing
8. Poetry workshop
9. Reflections on the unfamiliar
10. Guided mini-lessons

The level of significance in any activity is difficult to determine until *after* the experience is completed. Even the smallest activity can become imbued with the power to transform perception and to initiate deeper meaning when the participant is ready to receive the gifts inherent in the activity.

Part 11: Nonwriting Activities to Stimulate Writing

As part of pre-event preparation, participants and/or the facilitator can select and design nonwriting activities that are meant to stimulate on-site writing.[1] A few suggestions are listed below:

1. Cooking for a larger group of people
2. Creating a catalog of trees on site
3. Fishing
4. Swimming
5. Water testing of a nearby river, brook, or lake
6. Listing indigenous wildlife, birds, or insects
7. Listing edible food indigenous to the area, e.g., chamomile, mint, berries, or specific mushrooms
8. Observing animal tracks that were identified during a pre-event mini-lesson
9. Observing star constellations
10. Having a period of silent time
11. Practicing yoga
12 Analyzing group dynamics

Just about any activity during the event can be a subject for writing. Simply sitting quietly in one spot to observe the activity over a complete hour can produce interesting observations and reflections for writing journal entries, songs, poems, letters, and nonfiction.

REFERENCES

Bowers, C. A. (1995). The cultural dimensions of ecological literacy. *The Journal of Environmental Education, 27,* 5–10.

Hanna, G. (1995). Wilderness-related environmental outcomes of adventure and ecology educational programing. *The Journal of Environmental Education, 27,* 21–32.

Orr, D. (1992). *Ecological literacy: Education and the transition to a postmodern world.* Albany: State University of New York Press.

Roerden, L. P. (2001). Lessons of the wild (pp. 53–76). In L. Lantieri (Ed.), *Schools with spirit.* Boston: Beacon.

NOTE

1. A friend and colleague, Don Backus, told me of a meaningful outdoor activity he was assigned. The instructor took students to a nearby wooded area and placed them here and about, but well spaced apart from each other. Each student was told not to move and to rope off a one-square-foot area. They then observed all life occurring within that one square foot. Don said his awareness of the existing diversity within that small space led him to understand the sensitive but strong balance between ecosystems found in the woods, *and* that led him to reconsider the interconnections larger systems are built upon. Years after he had this experience, he still referred to it as one of his most meaningful educational experiences.

Appendix A: Selected Holistic Schools

PRIMARY AND SECONDARY SCHOOLS

United States

Arizona

The Kino School, Tucson: www.kino-school.org
Verde Valley School, Sedona: www.vvsaz.org

California

Berkeley Montessori School, Berkeley: www.bmsonline.org
Cedarwood Sudbury School, Santa Clara: www.cedarwoodsudbury.org/index.html
Marin Day Schools, Mill Valley: www.marindayschools.org
Oak Grove School, Ojai: www.oakgroveschool.com
Park Day School, Oakland: www.parkdayschool.org
Play Mountain Place, Los Angeles: www.playmountain.org
Saklan Valley School, Moraga: www.saklan.org
San Francisco Waldorf School, San Francisco: www.sfwaldorf.org
Tierra Pacifica Charter School, Santa Cruz: www.tierrapacifica.santacruz.k12.ca.us/index.html
The Woolman Semester, Nevada City: www.woolman.org/woolman.html

Colorado

Alpine Valley School, Wheat Ridge: www.alpinevalleyschool.com
Jefferson County Open School, Lakewood: jeffcoweb.jeffco.k12.co.us/high/jcos
The Living School, Boulder: www.livingschool.org

Connecticut

Grove School, Madison: www.groveschool.org

Iowa

Ideal Girls' School, Maharishi Vedic City (formerly part of Fairfield): www.idealgirlsschool.org

Maine

The Bay School, Blue Hill: www.bayschool.org
The Liberty School, Blue Hill: www.liberty-school.org
The New School, Kennebunk: www.tnsk.org

Massachusetts

Academy at Swift River, Cummington: www.swiftriver.com
Ephraim Curtis Middle School, Sudbury: www.sudbury.k12.ma.us/curtis/about.html
Middlesex School, Concord: www.mxschool.edu
North Star Center, Hadley: www.northstarteens.org

Michigan

Christian Montessori School of Ann Arbor, Ann Arbor: www.cmsaa.org/index.html
Clonlara Campus School, Ann Arbor: clonlara.org
Daycroft Montessori School, Ann Arbor: www.daycroft.org
The Detroit Waldorf School, Detroit: www.detroitwaldorf.com
Oakland Steiner School, Rochester Hills: www.oaklandsteiner.com
Stepping Stones, Grand Rapids: www.montessorimichigan.org

Minnesota

The Friends School of Minnesota, St. Paul: www.fsmn.org
The Second Foundation School, Minneapolis: www.sfs.pvt.k12.mn.us/index.html

New Hampshire

The Meeting School, Rindge: www.mv.com/ipusers/tms/index.php
St. Paul's School, Concord: www.sps.edu

New Jersey

The New School of Monmouth County, Holmdel: www.the-new-school.com

New Mexico

The Tutorial School, Santa Fe: pages.prodigy.net/tutorial
Yaxche Learning Center, Taos: www.yaxche.org

New York

Albany Free School, Albany: www.albanyfreeschool.com
The Scarsdale Alternative School, Scarsdale: www.scarsdaleschools.k12.ny.us/hs/Aschool

North Carolina

Evergreen Community Charter School, Asheville: www.evergreenccs.org
Follow the Child (FCM), Raleigh: www.followthechild.org/index.htm
Rainbow Mountain Children's School, Asheville: www.rmcs.org
Stone Mountain School, Black Mountain: www.stonemountainschool.com

Oregon

Blue Mountain School, Cottage Grove: www.bluemountainschool.com
Mount Bachelor Academy, Prineville: www.mtba.com/index.htm

Pennsylvania

The Circle School, Harrisburg: www.circleschool.org
Upattinas School & Resource Center, Glenmoore: www.upattinas.org

Rhode Island

Enki Education, Inc., Providence: www.enkieducation.org/index.htm

Tennessee

Knoxville Montessori School, Knoxville: www.korrnet.org/kms/index.html

Texas

Austin Waldorf School, Austin: www.austinwaldorf.org

Vermont

Burke Mountain Academy, East Burke: www.burkemtnacademy.org

Virginia

Blue Ridge Discovery School, Lynchburg: www.blueridgediscoveryschool.org
The New School of Northern Virginia, Fairfax: www.nsnva.pvt.k12.va.us
Reston Montessori School, Reston: montessori.velocitypack.com

Washington

Alger Learning Center/Independence High School, Sedro-Woolley: www.independent-learning.com
Puget Sound Community School, Seattle: www.pscs.org

International

Australia

Cape Byron Rudolf Steiner School, Ewingsdale, NSW: www.capebyronsteiner.nsw.edu.au
The Gap State High School, The Gap, Qld: thegapshs.qld.edu.au

The School of Total Education, Warwick, Qld: www.sote.qld.edu.au/about/keyfacts.html

Canada

Alan Howard Waldorf School, Toronto, ON: www.ahws.org
The Beach School, Toronto, ON: www.thebeachschool.org

New Zealand

Tamariki School, Christchurch: www.tamariki.school.nz

United Kingdom

The Abbotsholme School, Staffordshire, England: www.abbotsholme.com/default.asp
Brockwood Park School, Hampshire, England: www.brockwood.org.uk
The Rudolf Steiner School, South Devon, Devon, England: www.steiner-south-devon.org
The Steiner School at Middle Wood, Lancaster, England: www.middlewood.org.uk/middlewood.html

HOLISTIC COLLEGES

Antioch College, Yellow Springs, OH: www.antioch-college.edu
Bennington College, Bennington, VT: www.bennington.edu
Earlham College, Richmond, IN: www.earlham.edu
Fairhaven College, Bellingham, WA: www.wwu.edu/depts/fairhaven/index.html
Hampshire College, Amherst, MA: www.hampshire.edu
Maharishi University of Management, Fairfield, IA: www.mum.edu
Naropa University, Boulder, CO: www.naropa.edu
New College of California, San Francisco, CA: www.newcollege.edu
New School University, New York, NY: www.newschool.edu
Pendle Hill, Wallingford, PA: www.pendlehill.org
Reed College, Portland, OR: web.reed.edu
Schumacher College, Devon, United Kingdom: www.schumachercollege.org.uk

Appendix B: Rhetorical Aims and Organizational Strategies

AIMS

1. The *argumentative* aim seeks to convince someone to accept your point of view or beliefs about a particular idea or issue. It relies on logical factual information and almost always omits any reference to emotions or anecdotal information. When emotional information is used, it is then referred to as the persuasive aim because it generally is held to persuade while facts and logic are objective evidence that leads to readers' changing their position to those presented in the argument. In practice, argumentation and persuasion often become synonymous.
2. The *informative aim* provides information to the reader. It is most often used in reports and relies on explanations of facts. It omits arguments and opinions.
3. The *expressive aim* shows the writer's emotions. The writer's personal point of view directs the writing. Expressive writing is most often used in autobiography and in creative nonfiction.

ORGANIZATIONAL STRATEGIES (ALSO REFERRED TO AS RHETORICAL MODES)

1. *Definition* writing offers detailed information that defines. The focus can be on a single word, an idea, an issue, a person, a place. Definition relies on facts, and in some cases can include the writer's personal opinion. Depending on the topic, definition

can be purely objective or subjective. The concept *government*, for example, can be formally defined by looking at facts and types of governments people use; it can also be informally defined by describing what it means to the writer on a personal basis.
2. When using *illustration*, writers provide examples to illustrate or demonstrate their point.
3. *Classification* requires grouping together ideas, issues, or objects that are the same or very similar. For example, when discussing flowers, those that grow year after year without any new planting are classed as *perennials*, whereas those flowers that must be planted anew each spring or fall are classed as *annuals*. Edible parts of vegetables that grow underground, like carrots, potatoes, or onions, are classed as *root vegetables*.

   Writers identify the elements or characteristics that qualify their subject for one group or another.
4. When *description* is used in writing, writers choose to reveal how subjects look, feel, sound, and function in terms of their relationship in space.
5. *Comparison contrast* is used when writers want to demonstrate how things are the same or how they are different. When writers compare two things they look for the characteristics in each that are the same, and when they contrast those two things they look for characteristics that are different.
6. There are three types of *process analysis*: writing the steps down about how a person did something themselves; writing the steps down about how another person did something; and writing the steps down about how to do something. Process writing almost always involves step-by-step actions or instructions to follow.
7. In *analysis* writing, writers look at the parts of the whole in order to understand or make meaning about the whole. Analysis requires looking very closely at the parts and their relationship

to one another as well as to how they come together to make the whole.

NOTE

Expanded versions of the information in this appendix can be found in nearly every grammar handbook on the market.

Annotated Bibliography

Abra, J. (1997). *The motives for creative work*. Cresskill, NJ: Hampton.
Abra presents a fundamental orientation to the psychology of creativity, analyzing motivation, drive, competition, biological, and environmental sources.

Amabile, T. M. (1983). *The social psychology of creativity*. New York: Springer-Verlag.
This book presents an important scholarly study of intrinsic motivations in creativity studies.

Ashton-Warner, S. (1986). *Teacher*. New York: Simon & Schuster.
Ashton-Warner describes an innovative teaching process she used with Maori students in New Zealand. Creativity becomes the agent of change.

Bachelard, G. (1969). *The poetics of space*. Boston: Beacon.
Bachelard presents a phenomenological study of space and the ways it governs perspective.

Boden, M. A. (Ed.). (1994). *Dimensions of creativity*. Cambridge, MA: MIT Press.
This edited book is a scholarly collection of essays that explore creativity studies.

Bopp, J., Bopp, M., Brown, L., & Lane, P. (1984). *The sacred tree*. Alberta, Canada: Four Worlds Development Press.
The authors present a detailed presentation of various ways to understand and use the Medicine Wheel in daily life.

Bowers, C. A. (1995). The cultural dimensions of ecological literacy. *The Journal of Environmental Education, 27*, 5–10.
This opinion piece offers a critical perspective of David Orr's definitions and for ecological literacy. Bowers contextualizes definitions and understandings within a cultural episteme.

Brand, A. G., & Graves, R. L. (Eds.). (1994). *Presence of mind: Writing and the domain beyond the cognitive.* Portsmouth, NH: Boynton Cook.

This book is a collection of essays written by scholars in education and composition studies. The authors explore a range of innovative approaches to teaching writing that address the whole learner, multiple intelligences, and holistic ways of learning.

Foehr, R. P., & Schiller, S. A. (Eds.). (1997) *The spiritual side of writing: Releasing the learner's whole potential.* Portsmouth, NH: Heinemann/Boynton Cook.

The first full collection of essays within composition studies that explore spiritual approaches to writing. Philosophical and pedagogical information is included.

Gardner, H. (1983). *Frames of mind.* New York: Basic Books.

Gardner presents his theory and model of seven intelligences.

Gardner, H. (1994). The creators' patterns. In M. A. Boden (Ed.), *Dimensions of creativity* (pp. 143–158). Cambridge, MA: MIT Press.

Gardner overviews creativity studies, provides a definition of creativity, and uses seven cases—Freud, Einstein, Picasso, Stravinsky, Eliot, Graham, and Gandhi—that examine creative processes. A fuller view of these case studies are detailed in Gardner's 1993 book *The Creators of the Modern Era.*

Gifford, D. (1956, October). *The creative process in the classroom.* Paper presented at the Conference on Creativity as a Process, Arden House, Harriman, NY, October.

Gifford describes ways the creative process is evoked in classroom teaching.

Goleman, D. (1995). *Emotional intelligence.* New York: Bantam.

Goleman breaks new ground by defining and describing *emotional intelligence.* He makes an effective case for why it can be more important than IQ.

Goleman, D., Kaufman, P., & Ray, M. (1992). *The creative spirit.* New York: Penguin.

Inspired by the television show *The Creative Spirit,* this book persuades readers to believe that the creative spirit is in all of us and that a widespread creative renaissance is possible if people let the creative spirit infuse their life.

Goswami, A., & Goswami, M. (1999). *Quantum creativity: Waking up to our creative potential.* Cresskill, NJ: Hampton.

This book suggests that consciousness is the central theme of the universe and that "creativity is our lifeline to consciousness" (p. xv). It provides an integrated approach to all the various forms of creativity and looks closely at ways all people of all ages can realize their creative potential.

Greenberg, D. (1987). *Free at last: The Sudbury Valley School.* Framingham, MA: Sudbury Valley School Press.

Greenberg, teacher at Sudbury, writes a personal and descriptive overview of the first Sudbury School.

Hanna, G. (1995). Wilderness-related environmental outcomes of adventure and ecology educational programing. *The Journal of Environmental Education, 27*, 21–32.

This longitudinal research uses qualitative and quantitative measures to compare and contrast adventure education and ecology education programs. It suggests support for a holistic approach to bring about long-term change.

Harrison, S. (2002). *The happy child.* Boulder, CO: Sentient.

This book declares that education needs to be aimed at preserving and responding to the child's happiness. It criticizes the climate of competition and fear that prevails in compulsory and public education and supports developing community-based learning communities.

Juergensmeyer, M. (1984). *Gandhi's way: A handbook of conflict resolution.* Berkeley: University of California Press.

Juergensmeyer presents an overview of Gandhian theory and practice as well as case study results and solutions to some difficulties existing in the Gandhian approach to conflict resolution.

Kane, J. (2000). Waldorf education: Reflections on the essentials. In J. P. Miller & Y. Nakagawa (Eds.), *Education and the soul.* Albany: State University of New York Press.

Kane writes a thorough and detailed review of Waldorf education.

Kessler, R. (2000). *The soul of education.* Alexandria, VA: Association for Supervision and Curriculum Development.

This book presents seven gateways through which students might pass as a means to nourish soul and to stimulate the whole person. It presents a holistic model and calls for education reform at the local and national levels.

Kitchen, J. (Ed.). (2005). *Short takes: Brief encounters with contemporary nonfiction.* New York: Norton.

This collection features short contemporary essays that suit limited reading times.

Kumar, S. (2002). *You are, therefore I am: A declaration of dependence.* Devon, England: Green Books.

This book presents the spiritual journey of the author and presents a spiritual, philosophical, and practical view of holism that any person can use for daily living.

Lantieri, L. (Ed.). (2001). *Schools with spirit: Nurturing the inner lives of children and teachers.* Boston: Beacon.

Lantieri presents an excellent collection of essays focused on spiritual approaches to learning. A broad and nonreligious perspective dominates the work and invites an acceptance of spirit in schools.

Lantieri, L., & Patti, J. (1996). *Waging peace in our schools.* Boston: Beacon.

Peacekeeping and violence-prevention strategies and processes that have proven effective in schools are documented and supported by specific cases.

Lopate, P. (Ed.). (1995). *The art of the personal essay.* New York: Anchor.

This seminal collection features a broad range of essays that are organized by topic and genre.

McMahan, E., Funk, R., & Day, S. (1988). *The elements of writing about literature and film.* New York: Macmillan.

The authors present a brief overview of literary elements used in literature and film. Includes chapters on fiction, poetry, drama, and the writing process, and a glossary of definitions.

Mercogliano, C. (1998). *Making it up as we go along: The story of the Albany Free School.* Portsmouth, NH: Heinemann.

This book provides philosophy, history, and practice of a democratic approach to education as it is practiced at the Albany Free School. It offers alternatives to conventional mainstream education.

Meyers, P. (2003). K2. In J. Stanford (Ed.), *Responding to literature: Stories, poems, plays and essays* (4th ed., pp. 891–913). Boston: McGraw-Hill.

Two men, one injured, are trapped on a mountain at 27,000 feet. An argument follows as to why the able-bodied man should leave his friend alone to die.

Michalko, M. (2001). *Cracking creativity: The secrets of creative genius.* Berkeley, CA: Ten Speed.

This book provides a variety of practical and easy-to-use strategies for developing creativity in individuals.

Miller, J. P. (1993). *Holistic teacher.* Toronto: OISE Press.

The author offers guidelines and philosophy for becoming a holistic teacher.

Miller, J. P. (1996). *The holistic curriculum.* Toronto: OISE Press.
This book is an introduction to what a holistic curriculum contains and how it is facilitated. Theoretical and philosophical foundations are also provided.

Miller, J. P. (2000). *Education and the soul: Toward a spiritual curriculum.* Albany: State University of New York Press.
The first half presents historical and philosophical frames for addressing the soul in education. The second half describes practices a teacher might use in the classroom. This book is drawn from Miller's long career in holistic teaching.

Miller, J. P. (2006). *Educating for wisdom and compassion.* Thousand Oaks, CA: Corwin.
Theoretical and philosophical foundations, practice, and outcomes of this approach are described by Miller.

Miller, J. P., Karsten, S., Denton, D., Orr, D., & Colalillo Kates, I. (Eds.). (2005). *Holistic learning and spirituality in education: Breaking new ground.* Albany: State University of New York Press.
This collection of essays is based on conference presentations from the first three International Holistic Education conferences held in Toronto every two years.

Miller, J. P., & Nakagawa, Y. (2002). *Nurturing our wholeness: Perspectives on spirituality in education.* Brandon, VT: The Foundation for Educational Renewal.
A collection of essays that addresses traditions, teachers, and practices. This book broadens the discussion about secular spirituality in education.

Miller, R. (1997). *What are schools for? Holistic education in American culture* (3rd ed.). Brandon, VT: Holistic Education Press.
Political, philosophical, social, financial, cultural, and historical pressures that have caused holistic education to emerge are thoroughly discussed. This book provides an excellent starting point and introduction to the field of holistic education.

Miller, R. (1991). *New directions in education: Selections from holistic review.* Brandon, VT: Holistic Education Press.
This collection includes over 30 essays that were previously published in the journal *Holistic Education Review.* A broad range of topics articulating and demonstrating holistic principles are covered.

Miller, R. (Ed.). (2000). *Creating learning communities: Models, resources, and new ways of thinking about teaching and learning.* Brandon, VT: The Foundation for Educational Renewal.

This is an excellent introduction to alternative educational choices such as home schooling and community learning centers.

Mintz, J., Solomon, R., & Solomon, S. (Eds.). (1994). *The handbook of alternative education*. New York: Macmillan.

This is a resource directory that lists alternative schools. The first 30 pages describe and orient readers to alternative education. Four classifications include public choice, public at risk, independent (or private), and home-based.

Moffett, J. (1994). *The universal schoolhouse: Spiritual awakening through education*. San Francisco: Jossey-Bass.

One of the first full-length discussions about spiritual approaches in education.

Neill, A. S. (1992). *Summerhill school: A new view of childhood*. A. Lamb (Ed.). New York: St. Martin's Griffin.

Summerhill school established the traditions associated with the "Free School." It is the model from which many Free Schools arose. This book describes Summerhill and the people credited with beginning a revolutionary form of education.

Neville, B. (1989). *Educating psyche*. North Blackburn, Victoria, Australia: Collins Dove.

Neville persuades readers to reconstruct their view of education so that it moves beyond logic and rationality as primary teaching methods. Readers are encouraged to use auto-suggestion, visualization, positive affirmation, constructive imagining, the power of myths, metaphors, meditation, the relaxation response, and others.

Noddings, N. (1992). *The challenge to care in schools: An alternative approach to education*. New York: Teachers College Press.

Noddings presents a philosophy of "care" as a framework for educational reform. People learn best in an environment of caring that is based on support rather than on competition or evaluation.

Orr, D. (1992). *Ecological literacy: Education and the transition to a postmodern world*. Albany: State University of New York Press.

A seminal book that defines ecological literacy and offers theory and practice to encourage ecological literacy.

Palmer, P. J. (1998). *The courage to teach: Exploring the inner landscape of a teacher's life*. San Francisco: Jossey-Bass.

This book explores why teachers teach and why personal rejuvenation and professional development must come from the heart.

Rocha, D., & DeSouza, L. (2003). *Schools where children matter: Exploring educational alternatives.* Brandon, VT: The Foundation for Educational Renewal.

Three holistic schools are profiled with praise and criticism. Parents, teachers, and students are interviewed.

Roerden, L. P. (2001). Lessons of the wild. In L. Lantieri (Ed.), *Schools with spirit* (pp. 53–76). Boston: Beacon.

This essay documents an outdoor learning program that takes students to scuba dive "the wall" off the Grand Cayman Island.

Root, R. L., Jr., & Steinberg, M. (Eds.). (2005). *The fourth genre: Contemporary writers of/on creative nonfiction* (3rd ed.). New York: Pearson Longman.

An edited collection of creative nonfiction essays that can be used as models for readers and writers of nonfiction. The introduction contains a thorough philosophical, theoretical, and practical overview of the genre.

Simmons, G. (2003). *The I of the storm: Embracing conflict, creating peace.* Unity Village, MO: Unity House.

A process that leads to peacemaking teaches us how to embrace conflict and to use it within the process. The spiritual self, the "I" of the storm, lies at the center of this approach, which also integrates a variety of spiritual and scientific concepts.

Tompkins, J. (1996). *A life in school: What the teacher learned.* Reading, MA: Perseus.

Tompkins writes a memoir of her years in school. It calls for the need for a holistic approach to education.

Vaughan, F. (1986). *The inward arc: Healing and wholeness in psychotherapy and spirituality.* Boston: Shambhala.

This book came to be the foundational text for transpersonal psychology. It takes a holistic approach to promote self-healing. Vaughan posits that spirituality and psychotherapy are complementary.

About the Author

Susan A. Schiller, PhD, is a professor of English and member of the Graduate Faculty at Central Michigan University. She teaches composition, American literature, film studies, and English education. Her research interests include spiritual approaches to writing and learning, holistic education, studies in Willa Cather, and imagery and affect in meaning making. She has published in *Journal of the Assembly for Expanded Perspectives on Learning*, *Innovative Higher Education*, *Transformations*, and *Language Arts Journal of Michigan*. She coedited, with Regina Paxton Foehr, a collection of essays titled *The Spiritual Side of Writing: Releasing the Learner's Whole Potential* and cochaired, with Robert Root, a national conference for AEPL titled "Mapping Nonfiction." She lives in Mt. Pleasant, Michigan, with her husband Theopolis L. Gilmore.

www.ingramcontent.com/pod-product-compliance
Lightning Source LLC
Chambersburg PA
CBHW021852300426
44115CB00005B/129